Praise for
Behind the Hidden Doors

I was holding back tears after just the foreword. As a mama with littles just starting to reach the age of potential bullying, I could feel the pain and emotion of knowing your child is hurting through the words in this book. I pictured my daughter, feeling as though the world hated her, and felt a rush of instant protection over her. I believe this book is a Godsend to parents, not just living it but also *before* experiencing bullying issues—so that we can be aware of the signs, struggles, and behaviors that may alert us that our child is being bullied. Taking assertive advice and encouragement from a mama who has experienced it firsthand and through her babies gives her the ultimate authority to guide and empower other parents to take their child's life back into their own hands and God's. There is a rattling and terrifying trend of seeing very young children take their lives because of bullying. It is not to be underestimated. *Behind the Hidden Doors* can literally save the lives of many children and the homes of many families.

Lindsey Graham, The Patriot Barbie, mom, political activist, author, entrepreneur, and influential speaker

Bullying is not isolated to a specific demographic or socioeconomic status, it can touch anyone at any time; no one is exempt. Having been bullied myself as a young girl, and unfortunately having observed the disheartening experiences each of my three children had with being bullied by peers—and in one case, the worst case, a teacher—I've seen the negative impacts of bullying. It can be isolating and debilitating and knows no boundaries regarding long-term effects on mental health. As a parent, it is overwhelming and heartbreaking to watch your child suffer at the hands of another child or teacher, especially when you feel incapable of saying and doing the right things. *Behind the Hidden Doors* is a blessing for all parents facing the pain of their child's suffering under the injustice of bullying. It is a must-read for parents and teachers to aid in recognizing a child's suffering and to help them navigate the emotions and the unhealthy environment they are often subjected to tolerate.

Dr. Robyn Graham, best-selling author of *You, Me, and Anxiety: Take Action Over Anxiety to Enjoy Being You*

Rachel Rector shares openly about her daughter's experience with bullying to provide the reader with a sense of understanding, belonging, and hope in the midst of all the emotions they may be experiencing. She thoroughly provides insights on how to listen to a child who has been bullied and how to find the resources to support them. Rachel writes from her heart, filled with the Holy Spirit to encourage the reader each step along the way.

Christina Smith, MA, licensed professional counselor, trauma-informed counselor

Behind the Hidden Doors is a much-needed and valuable resource for parents and caregivers navigating the challenge of childhood bullying. No parent wants to see their child hurting, and the feeling of powerlessness is the most frustrating. This book clearly lays out the signs and remedies any parent can rely on. Having survived bullying and experienced it with my children, I would have loved this shortcut guide to help make the journey easier. When we place our children at the feet of Jesus and look to Him for wisdom, both parents and children can come out of this experience stronger for God's glory!

Mimika Cooney, author of multiple books, including award-winning *Unstick Your Mind: Shift Your Mindset, Develop Grit & Break Barriers,* bestselling *Mindset Make Over,* and *Worrier to Warrior: A Mother's Journey from Fear to Faith*

In *Behind the Hidden Doors*, Rachel Rector has given moms a means of understanding and communicating about the reality of hard relationships with our children. Rector offers a blend of biblical truth, clear language, and practical suggestions for guiding our children through the difficult encounters they will undoubtedly face with others. This is a resource all parents will find deeply encouraging and profoundly useful.

Teri Lynne Underwood, MAEd, author of *Praying for Girls: Asking God for the Things They Need Most*

As a mom of three children of twenty-seven years and a trauma-informed professional, *Behind the Hidden Doors: Bullying, Hope, and Identity* immediately pierced my heart. I must admit that I feel that my oldest child may have been bullied, but he was so quiet, and I was so distracted by my own hurt I did not see it until it had already stopped. But with my middle child, it was clear. She was bullied from first grade to fourth grade. I wish I knew of or had a resource like *Behind the Hidden Doors*. It is a much-needed source for parents, children, families, and communities, encouraging and empowering them. We know that bullying can make someone feel that they do not belong. If we do not feel we belong, we are at an increased risk for numerous vulnerabilities.

Tori J. Jones, community engagement manager, Freekind

Rachel Rector does an amazing job getting to the heart of her reader with both encouraging words and applicable guidance. *Behind the Hidden Doors* teaches the effects of bullying, the signs of bullying, and just how to navigate all this with your child as their advocate. This book is an amazing resource for teachers, counselors, guardians, and *you*, the mama, to have on the shelf!

Liz Andersen, Love Remained Ministries

BEHIND
THE HIDDEN DOORS

Best Selling Author Rachel Rector

BEHIND
THE HIDDEN DOORS

RACHEL RECTOR

Behind Hidden Doors: Bullying, Hope, and Identity

Copyright 2024 © Rachel Rector

All information, techniques, ideas and concepts contained within this publication are of the nature of general comment only and are not in any way recommended as individual advice. The intent is to offer a variety of information to provide a wider range of choices now and in the future, recognizing that we all have widely diverse circumstances and viewpoints. Should any reader choose to make use of the information contained herein, this is their decision, and the contributors (and their companies), authors and publishers do not assume any responsibilities whatsoever under any condition or circumstances. It is recommended that the reader obtain their own independent advice.

Scripture taken from THE HOLY BIBLE, NEW INTERNATIONAL VERSION (NIV)®. Copyright© 1973, 1978, 1984, 2011 by Biblica, Inc.™. Used by permission of Zondervan.

First Edition 2024

All rights reserved in all media. No part of this book may be used, copied, reproduced, presented, stored, communicated or transmitted in any form by any means without prior written permission, except in the case of brief quotations embodied in critical articles and reviews.

The moral right of Rachel Rector as the author of this work has been asserted by her in accordance with the Copyrights, Designs and Patents Act of 1988.

Published by F.I.T. in Faith Press

To my sweet Madison: Until this journey, I didn't know what the extent of your name would mean—"Gift from God and Mighty Warrior." I know this healing journey has been beyond challenging, but I am so proud of all the hard work you've put into finding yourself again and walking in truth and freedom! Thank you for being willing to share pieces of your journey and help survivors after you.

To you, the parent or advocate, and all the bullying survivors who've opened this book: I commend your bravery for holding on to hope and finding the tools you need to rise again. Standing with you and cheering you on as you find healing, hope, and identity again!

And all the survivors and families who come after us: Praying this becomes a movement as we join forces, stand together, and change the trajectory of schools!

Contents

Acknowledgments xiii
Foreword... xvii
Introduction 1

1 Home Front Door 11

2 School Entrance Door 17

3 The Attic—*Into the Child's Mind* 31

4 Living Room Door 35

5 Home Office Door 51

6 Counselor's Office Door 61

7 Classroom Door 75

8 Administrator's Door 85

9 Primary Bedroom Door 103

10 Child's Bedroom Door 119

11 Child's Bathroom Door 129

Afterword—*A Survivor's Testimony* 141
Endnotes 149
About the Author 153
Recommended Resources 155
Next Steps 159

Acknowledgments

I am grateful to my dad, Kevin Wickey, for believing in me and this movement and allowing *Behind the Hidden Doors* to be birthed into the world. Without your support and your weekly encouragement, Dad, this book would not have been possible and wouldn't be a resource in the hands of the current readers and readers to come. Thank you for your love, support, and your continual encouragement! Thank you for calling me one day and saying, "What will it take to get this book published this year? *Now* is the time, Rach! The world needs it *today*!"

To Tamra Andress and the F.I.T. in Faith Press team, thank you for seeing the vision of what *Behind the Hidden Doors* should be, where it should go, and the hands that need to open it up and implement the action steps provided inside. You knew the world needed this from the moment I shared my desire to attend your author retreat. You continued to envision it and cheer me on, especially on the days I wanted to give up. I am forever appreciative of your partnership as this launches into the world! In addition, thank you, Tamra, for delving into your trauma to shed light in the foreword on other areas that need to come into the open for many families to feel seen and heard in their journeys.

To my editor, Cortney Donelson, a sincere thank you for helping me grow as a writer and bringing this book to life! You are like a makeup artist. You look at the creation before you and see all its beautiful attributes and personality. Then, with a little bit of this and a lot of that, you fancy it up and leave it more radiant than before it came to you. Thank you for seeing my vision and words and meeting the reader right where she is, with the perfect choice of words she needed to hear. In addition, thank you for your encouragement and for helping me no longer dislike the red editing pen and instead see how the necessary edits bring the story to life.

To my husband, Jeremy Rector—wow, this was a wild ride, wasn't it? Thank you for staying married to me during the long-suffering journey of healing for our daughter and then reliving many pieces of the trauma again as we brought them into the light for these readers and their children who need a guide on their healing journeys. I am gratified by the many hours you took our children outside or allowed me to leave the house to get these words onto the pages. You saw this through from the moment I shared God's dream and vision with you, and you continued to gently push me on the days I wanted to throw in the towel because I knew I was missing out on family time to bring this to fruition.

Christina Smith, you were a Godsend when you said yes to counseling Madison. You always greeted us with a smile and made us feel safe during our weeks with you as we shared all the emotions, hurts, events, and things that happened. You never judged me as a parent. Instead, you listened intently and gave me tools and strategies to meet my daughter where she was and gently nudged her to the next step to take in her trauma and navigate her healing journey. You brought my daughter's light, joy, worth, identity, and self-confidence back, for which I will forever be indebted to you! We were both so sad the day we had to say, "See you later," but you reassured us it wasn't a goodbye and that you were praying the best for us! The majority of the tools I share in the "Counselor's Office Door" chapter and the "Child's Bedroom Door" chapter and the idea of the I Am statements paired with Scripture were first shared by you. Overall, without your support and advocacy for our daughter, this book would never have been created and published because my daughter and I wouldn't have learned the tools we needed to bring her back and keep *hope* alive throughout her journey. Thus,

Acknowledgments

we wouldn't have had any joy, hope, and energy to share with the readers.

To Rose Lubbert, my mom, and to Grandma, thank you for the guidance, discipline, and prayer you provided for Madison on her healing journey when I had nothing left to give. You allowed space, love, and kindness for me and her—always free of judgment on some of the darkest days we experienced. In addition, you gifted your quiet home to me and allowed me countless hours during the beginning stages of this book, where I could listen to worship music and cry while the words flowed through my typing fingers.

To my ride-or-die friends and women's Bible study friends in Nebraska and Virginia, you prayed *Behind the Hidden Doors* into existence. You cried with me on the hard days and sent encouragement to help me put one foot in front of the other. You celebrated me during the small and big wins. One of you even took time out of your workday to attend my first keynote speech on this book before it was published. People say, "It takes a village" to live life well, raise children properly, and live abundantly on this side of heaven. My heart is so full knowing that you are my village, you chose me, you see me, you hear me, and you still want to be a part of my life with a smile!

Morgan Hart, I specifically wanted to thank you by name. You prayed for my family through some of the scariest and darkest moments I don't care to ever experience again. You willingly read and replied to every text or phone call I sent during the valley moments, all without judgment. You aren't afraid to give me a quick kick in the pants when I am dwelling on the emotions or something mentally, and you always bring me and what I am going through back to the Word, prayer, and Jesus. Additionally, you celebrate with me during all levels of wins in business, life, and, most importantly, faith. Whenever we meet up, the hours on the clock fly by, and they only seem like minutes. You see and hear the good, the bad, and the ugly, and you still call me "friend," always with a gentle smile.

To my sweet spiritual mentor, Donna Lopardo, you joined me on the second half of this author journey. The moment you shared during our Bible study time what God showed you in Scripture that week, I knew I couldn't wait to get to know you. As time passed, God nudged me to ask you to mentor me spiritually. I dug my heels in for months, thinking you would say no. Then the right opportunity came, God shoved me, and I asked you. You were honored with the ask but stated you needed to seek the Lord before answering. I knew from that response that once you said yes, I would be blessed and consider it a joy every time we met.

Finally, to my four children, I am thankful for the time you gifted me to sit down and write and get the message out that God wanted me to share. You lost many hours of "Mom time," but you smiled and excitedly reminded me, "My mom is going to be an author. That is so cool!" My prayer is that this is only the beginning for you, your generation, and all the generations to follow. May this be a movement that will reshape schools, the education system, teaching colleges and universities, and the government, from the state level to the nation as a whole! We must do better! We will do better! It takes *all* of us banning together and saying, "Enough is enough!"

Foreword

My stomach had butterflies every morning as I prepared to make my half-block walk to the bus stop. But not the kind you'd think a sixth-grade middle school girl would have. These were "fear flies," and I couldn't seem to get rid of them, no matter how much encouragement my parents gave me or even how much head knowledge I had, telling me they were just "mean girls." Constantly chanting hopeful messages to myself that they wouldn't hurt me, I found myself unprotected even in the first seat behind the school bus driver, where the two bigger, stronger, faster, not-so-kind eighth graders conjured up a way to get off at the same stop as me. I was in tears, pleading with the bus driver, trying to convince her they didn't have the appropriate parent note to get off there, but I didn't win the argument. She let them do what they wanted, and I started a full-out sprint home only after they grabbed my bookbag and pulled me backward.

Their belittling words and evil grins lingered in my spirit day by day. I begged for car rides to school. I no longer hung out at the bus stop. I waited until the final minute to pass the street and get on board. I would sit up front with friends who were smaller and younger and keep the back-seat bullies' attention off of me. All I knew to do was stay away and mind my own business. And surely, I recited, "Sticks and stones may break my bones, but words will never hurt me" in my head, but their meaning never landed in my heart.

You may have already painted the picture of a meek, calm-mannered, perhaps petite girl with braces, glasses, tattered hair, or hand-me-down clothes that hung on her tiny frame. Who knows how consumed media has distorted your mind as you think about the victim versus the child who is bullying, but my situation did not look like that, which is precisely why I tried to keep my emotions at bay, put on a brave face, and chose not to confide in teachers or get any parents involved. I was a cheerleader and involved in student government, which made me a "goody-two-shoes." The mean girls weren't the most popular; they were the outcasts who hid in the shadows. They were double my size and had language and habits I had never heard of to back up their antics and fear tactics. The only thing that made sense was the persistent narrative from my parents that "they're just jealous." I clung to that, which sadly fed my ego more than comforted me, but it helped enough to emulate a false confidence that kept me somewhat safe.

I didn't have "a friend in Jesus" at the time. So I never thought to pray. There was no comfort in knowing I had a Defender or Protector. There were no mantras or daily affirmations to chant, no podcasts or resources to google, "How to get rid of bullies." No children's books to read. But I did have, Arthur the Aardvark and his bunny buddy and friends (a morning cartoon that blasted daily from the TV and over my breakfast). It provided a comforting narrative that I wasn't the only one facing these trials. Ultimately, though, in the flesh, I really only had me and my not-so-comforting fear flies to keep me company.

Eventually, those girls graduated to high school and had two years to either pick on someone their own size or be taught what it feels like to be a small fish in a big pond. Luckily, when I arrived at the same high school after those two years, I had a built-in protection plan in my big sis, who drove me to school regularly. We passed that bus stop, and I felt in full control, with an assurance that running into them wouldn't be a concern—and even if it were, I had a whole army of supporters since my sister was a senior.

Interestingly, there was no real resolve, just this core memory.

Fast-forward a decade and a half later when I started down the journey of self-development, emotional intelligence, and the faith walk that forever changed my lens of empathy toward others. To be honest, I hadn't thought much of that scenario at all—besides movie moments that triggered the stuffed Pandora's closet I had been opening weekly through therapy sessions during this season of life.

The scenario that had me finally face the situation and extract the root pain to develop a healthy narrative around the girls I harbored resentment and unforgiveness toward unfolded in a Chick-fil-A play zone. This time, my role was Mama-bear, and I was confronted by my tearful four-year-old boy, who was being taunted by the older kids about his long hair. They were publicly humiliating him by insisting he "must be a girl." Luckily, claws didn't come out for those little cubs, but I did have a new understanding and a deeper lens of compassion to pour out and support the other kids in their limited perspective and persistent false words. I may have taken on a bit of a *tone* as I spoke about kindness as the emotions of my younger years surfaced, but they were playing together by the end. However, the earlier mentioned mantra was not my go-to because, in my wisdom, I knew words *do* hurt and feelings *aren't* forgotten, even when you forgive.

My son, to this day, faces that false narrative because of his sweet face and long hair. Mind you he's also a world-champ jujitsu player, so long hair is part of that culture. But now, with consistent support, he's carrying tools to combat the lies and a confidence in Christ that keeps him rooted in the Truth about who He is. Now it's a roll of the eyes and a quick response, saying, "Nope, I'm a boy." We won't go into the extension of the conversation connected to the gender identity issue, but you can be assured I've faced those conversations, too, as I fight for Truth and ensure the protection of my beautiful boy.

These resources weren't something I read in a manual or parent guide. I didn't have a signed anti-bullying contract for playgrounds. And parents, more often than not, haven't gone through the same social, emotional, relational, or communication coaching I have.

So why even share my story? Why does something so trivial even matter? I think the answer lies less in the testimony and trial and more in the effort to overcome and create safe spaces for everyone to become the best versions of themselves. No matter where you find yourself inside the story, even as a bystander, we all have the responsibility to stand up for justice, goodness, kindness, and love.

So what do we do as parents? As educators? As coaches and mentors and neighbors, even?

We realize everyone won't pick up a book like this because perhaps it's not the forward-facing problem they are encountering, but there is always a consistent evolution of conversation that needs to be aired. There are ethnic bullies, political and religious bullies, workplace bullies, and more, even (especially) in adulthood. So no one is excluded from this necessary narrative of hope, one that encourages us toward a shifted mindset concerning community and the benefits of rich connections as human beings.

From communications support to emotional development and relational strategy, *Behind the Hidden Doors* isn't a one-time, exclusive read. It's a lifetime weapon and a movement. You're invited to get on the good side of the fight. The one that supports every party involved. The one that looks to the roots of the problem instead of the child who is bullying as bad and the victim as *helpless*. There are deep-seated needs of everyone involved, and brushing the conversation under the rug or ignoring it as a "season" or situational circumstance that will eventually go away will never fix the core problems.

Hosea 4:6 declares, "My people are destroyed from lack of knowledge. Because you have rejected knowledge, I also reject you as my priests; because you have ignored the law of your God, I also will ignore your children."

This is an opportunity to do the deeper work. And it's way cheaper than years of therapy, though I highly recommend that too.

This resource will equip us and everyone involved in this issue, to move forward on one accord—and not just to sugarcoat the sour situation but to truly fix it and teach our youth how to establish healthy communication around hard topics while also prioritizing relational capital and long-term mental health.

I honor you, the reader, for being one of the brave ones willing to go beyond the cookie-cutter solution and truly be a champion for an often silent struggle. You are the change-makers this world needs.

Tamra Andress, international speaker, best-selling author, top 1-percent podcaster, marketplace minister

Introduction

All of my children slept, and my house was *finally* quiet. My weary body plopped into bed, and my head melted into my pillow, ready for a good night's rest. Just when I thought I could relax, the thoughts of the day came rushing like a river. Why is my daughter not talking to me? Why is she *so* mean to her brothers all of a sudden? Why is she yelling at me? Why won't she share about her day anymore? Did I do something to make her mad? Why is she so angry with me, spewing such mean words? Where are the meltdowns coming from? She is not a toddler anymore! Where did my kind, compassionate, sweet girl go? Then the salty tears rolled down my face like a waterfall, and my mind swirled with damaging thoughts, much like a destructive tornado.

As the endless questions crashed around in my mind, I heard a voice in the far distance whispering, "Rachel, Rachel, Rachel . . . why are you crying?"

Forgetting I was deep in thought, I jumped, figuring out it was my husband whispering to me in the night. I glanced at him and blubbered through the tears, "I just don't understand! Madison seems so dark now. I pick her up from school, and the drive home is eerily quiet. The moment she walks through the door, it's like a light is switched on, and she turns into a monster. She pushes her brothers, yells at the top of her lungs, screams at me for the littlest things, and rarely smiles." I sighed. "It's like she is mad at the world, and I don't know why. She has always been an open book. She used to talk my ear off from sun up to sun down, even tattling on herself if she did something wrong. What am I doing wrong as a mama? There seems to be a dark cloud following her around."

While searching for answers, we concluded I was doing nothing wrong as a mama, but we had no idea where all this was coming from. The only notion we agreed on was that maybe she just missed her best friends—one who had moved away and another who no longer went to her private school. With their absence, maybe she was having a hard time adjusting to fourth grade and figuring out who she could play with during recess. She had always been a reserved child who hated change, and it took her time to develop friendships.

The rest of the evening played in my mind like a movie reel. Wait! Stop right there! I thought, *Right before bed, our daughter stomped down the hall in haste, yelling, "No one likes me," "Everyone hates me!" then "I'm the worst person in the world!" and "I wish I wasn't alive!"* I leaned over to my husband, who was now sleeping, and shakily cried, "She yelled, 'I wish I wasn't alive!'" As a teacher, I'd had suicide training. How had I missed this? "Oh no, do you think she really means that?" I'd read about elementary students taking their lives. "Do you think she would do that?" *Would she even know how? This frightened me!*

The tornado in my mind picked up speed again, and all the stories I'd heard about childhood suicide flashed before my eyes. Would our daughter be the next story? *I can't lose my daughter! I don't want to lose my daughter.* She had so much more life to live. I knew God had a plan for her life, and it couldn't be His will to end at nine years old. Thinking something is one thing, but verbalizing it made it even more real!

As I came out of my head and shared the thoughts that were swirling inside of me, tears welled up in my husband's eyes, his face turned downcast, and we agreed we did not want this to be the end of our daughter's story. We prayed for her mind to be sound, her actions to be pure, truth to be revealed, and help to be found—and for her safety.

Introduction

After saying *Amen*, I tiptoed to her bedroom and saw a shadow of her through the cracked opening in her door. I quietly opened it and gazed upon her face. It spoke of so much pain from her day. Pain I knew nothing about yet. I knelt beside her bed and watched her breathe as her chest went up and down. Up and down. Up and down. *Thank you that she is still breathing!* I did not want to arouse her from her sleep. Sleep she so desperately needed. I do not remember the exact blessing or prayer I prayed over her, but I do remember, with my tear-stained face, whispering over her. "God, please keep this precious child safe! Please let her know she is fearfully and wonderfully made." After a short time, it took every ounce of strength I could muster to leave her side and crawl back to my pillow.

It was so hard to go to sleep that night. My brain had a difficult time shutting off the tornado swirl to allow me to fall asleep. By the grace of God, I finally fell asleep hours later, knowing she was on the other side of our bedroom wall, and that somehow, God loved her more than me (even though I still struggled to fathom the multitude of that love).

This is where our journey began. I am not going to sugarcoat it. This journey was beyond challenging, and many times, I felt isolated and alone. Nothing prepares a mama for the helplessness and lack of control she feels when learning that her child is or has been bullied. I am a mama who has been through the heartache and fear of worrying that my daughter would take her life because of the mean words and actions of her peers.

I hope to lessen some of the blow for you and save you from some of the heartache we went through. I desire to create a bridge for you and your child, one to support you as you find healing, hope, and identity and as you unlock the doors of bullying and walk in redemption—not only for your child but also for your mama's heart.

Layout of *Behind the Hidden Doors*

Have you ever been to a museum or a foreign country and had a guide walk you through each room, down each street, or past each precious landmark? Well, just like that guide, I am going to walk through several doors with you as light shines into each room of your child's bullying story (at home, school, and some offices). Just like a museum or foreign country's guide, I am here to lead the way, share important information to get you through safely, encourage you to ask more questions, reveal things that only a local or professional guide would know (as a fellow parent of a bullying survivor), and take your hand when it gets hard or dark. You are not meant to do this alone! Before we officially walk through each door, I will prepare you for what you might experience when you enter. And we will walk through that room *together*.

At the end of each room (i.e., chapter), you will take a deep breath in and a deep breath out. You will reflect on what you experienced in that particular room, and we will prepare for the next door you will unlock and walk through. If at any time you feel like we are going too fast or you are overwhelmed, then, just like you would with a real-life guide, tell me you need to pause. Reach out to me using the QR code in the back of the book, and we will pause together. We will reflect on what is causing you to feel overwhelmed—or talk through whatever emotion has come up—so you can move on to the next room.

I walked this journey alone and do not want that for you. We were meant to live life in community, and I would be honored to play a small role in your bigger community. However, I am *not* a licensed counselor, so if you are feeling deep emotions, like anxiety or depression, or it feels too dark and all-consuming, I highly encourage you to reach out to a trained, professional counselor.

One chapter can help you, specifically as a parent, refuel, recharge, and restore yourself. That chapter is called "Primary Bedroom Door." If you are feeling depleted or exhausted, or you just

Introduction

need to refuel your mind, body, or spirit, feel free to skip ahead and walk through that door. This is a resource book, so you do not need to read it cover to cover, in the order I wrote it. It is written in the order that chronologically follows our bullying journey. However, as I share later, some doors are meant to be walked through multiple times in your journey to healing. There is no shame in entering a room more than once, and there is no right or wrong way to walk through this resource. Your journey is unique, just like your child is uniquely precious; therefore, the doors will be opened in the order that matches your child, you, and your family. I walked through some of these doors multiple times. However, for the sake of space and so that you don't feel like you are carrying around an encyclopedia (yes, I just aged myself!), I only dedicated one chapter per room. I included the meat and potatoes of each room, but, of course, there is always room for gravy, sauce, or spices as you walk back through the doors a second, third, or fourth time. Don't feel like you have to run through each of these chapters. Instead, I challenge you to first look around, just like you would at a museum or in a spectacular foreign city, absorbing all the sights and then reflecting on each experience as you feel more comfortable.

Gender and Terms

In *Behind the Hidden Doors*, I refer to a child being bullied as "she" or "her." I am doing this so any understanding is not lost and the language can be more easily understood. However, I know both male and female students are bullied every day, and both genders can also be the child who is doing the bullying. I not only have a daughter, but I am also a mom of three boys. I know the negative words that can be spoken over them and the physical actions that can be taken against them. Boys are not exempt from being bullied. I have had both a daughter and a son experience bullying in primary school, so I know being bullied is not bound by gender. Each gender is equally human; both can be hurt or be the ones causing the hurt. As parents, you need to advocate equally for both genders and not allow them to be bullied because "boys will be boys" or "girls at that age are just mean." Those are excuses and do not bring about solutions. However, for the remainder of this book, the child being bullied will be referred to using female pronouns for the sake of clarity.

Some of the terms I use in this book are only used for ease of reading. I do not think children should receive or accept these titles, and they should not be carried with them for the rest of their lives. For example, I will say "bully" types in one chapter. I use this term so you can understand who I am describing. However, as I will mention in "Administrator's Door," no child should have the title "bully" spoken over them for life. Children are moldable and, in the right adult hands, I hope children who choose to bully will be seen in a new light. These are students crying out in the wrong ways and for several reasons, which we will discuss. Therefore, teachers and administrators should hold them accountable for their actions and give them consequences for their behaviors, *but* they also need to find the root causes for why the child is acting in this manner and teach them new ways and patterns that will get them to stop bullying their peers.

A term that I will not use is *victim*. The only time you will see that word in this book is when I reference another professional who used it in his work, which I've quoted. I wholeheartedly believe children who have been bullied are "survivors." By wearing the title of "victim," a child loses her power and identity over her life, and that is exactly what we *do not* want for

> **We get to choose to rise from the ashes and live in the truth of who we are, walk in freedom, and not let the past define and dictate who we are in the present and future!**

our children. We want our children to hold the power of their lives in their hands instead of giving it away to their peers and others. Please hear me when I say *I am in no way downplaying the pain that a survivor of bullying has endured.* Trust me. I have walked the painful road with our children, especially our daughter. Yet, as I taught her, we get to choose to rise from the ashes and live in the truth of who we are, walk in freedom, and not let the past define and dictate who we are in the present and future!

Another term you will see in this book is *Mama*. This word is used for ease of reading, but it is referring to anyone reading this book. *Behind the Hidden Doors* is for any caregiver who wants to advocate for a child. It is for the parents or other adults willing to roll up their sleeves and do the dirty work to bring back their children's hope, identity, worth, and value. My husband was an additional advocate and warrior for my child. Thus, I know that male or female, mom or dad, grandma or grandpa, uncle or aunt, guardian, strong mentor, adult sibling, or whatever loving adult wants to help the child being bullied rise again, will benefit from my story and this information. It takes a village to raise a child—and an even bigger village to wage war and fight for the child whose voice is not being heard or upheld. No matter your gender, your role in a child's life, your marital status, or your biological or nonbiological makeup and connection to the child, I commend you for seeing her worth! In addition, I am proud of you for acknowledging you need more information, more tools or weapons, and for being willing to invest the money and time to purchase and read *Behind the Hidden Doors* and get the help the child in your life needs.

Map of the Book

Just like a museum guide shares the rules, guidelines, and map of the museum, I, your bullying guide on your healing journey, will do the same. The first two chapters define what bullying is; the difference between the words *bullying*, *mean*, and *rude*; the types of bullying and what they look like; and common behaviors survivors show when being bullied. They are purposeful in helping you know how a child is being bullied, why the child is exhibiting certain behaviors, and what correct verbiage and documentation to use when you advocate for the child. Bullying is a sensitive topic and a heated word in the school system, and I want you to use it correctly and be "armored up" as you go to battle for your child's life, identity, and future. The last thing I want for you is to go into the school and be completely shut down by teachers, administrators, and staff because of a lack of knowledge or misusing words when sharing about your child's situation and what they have experienced. Instead, I want you to come out victorious for your child, to help her gain back her hope, worth, and identity—to not just survive but thrive!

As we consider museums, we might realize no two people walk through a museum the same way. *Behind the Hidden Doors* is no different. Many will start at the beginning and work through from the first chapter to the final chapter. However, you may need to start in the middle and then jump back to the beginning for some definitions or clarity on certain topics. Then, you might go back to the middle and continue reading. Others may think, *I know my child needs a counselor now, so I need to jump to the "Home Office Door" and browse the Factors to Consider When Choosing a Counselor.* Others may say their child is acting out and has huge emotions, and they are at their wits' end, with no clue what is going on in their child's head. Therefore, that parent needs to read, "The Attic" to get a glimpse into the turmoil that may be swirling around in their child's brain.

A disclaimer, though: I, of course, cannot and did not get in each of your child's heads. The exact workings of your child's brain and behavior will not be unveiled in "The Attic," but I give you a peek inside my daughter's brain from what she shared and experienced and what I know to be true to uncover what you may not even think *could* be going on in a child's mind (this was my favorite chapter to write). If at any point you feel discouraged, flip ahead to the Afterword and hear some more about my daughter's journey, including what she says to parents, teachers, and administrators after moving through her healing journey. In addition, I am always an email away, and I will be your biggest cheerleader, supporter, and encourager for your child's healing journey, where she will declare with gusto the survivor she is on the other side!

Your tour starts now! Grab a flashlight, walking shoes, water, some tissues, and a pen and paper. Flip the page and follow me through all these Hidden Doors. Some we will go through quickly and quietly, while with others, we will stay and look around for a while. Move at your own pace but don't stay behind too long in one room. You don't want to get lost in the darkness and lose out on finding the light and treasures in the rooms ahead. Let's forge ahead in this healing journey together—starting with taking your first big step now! Let's GO!

Home Front Door

As your child walks through the front door, your home becomes a safety zone for her. I know this. After all, you are reading *Behind the Hidden Doors* because you care deeply about your child. However, you may be wondering, *Why does my child blow up, meltdown, throw a tantrum, or* _____ *[fill in the blank] when she gets home?*

As a child enters her home, she feels safe and lets her guard down. She knows she is loved and will not be judged for immature responses to the world around her. Most of the time, a child acts out because she doesn't know how to tell you what is happening. Sometimes, she doesn't even know why she is feeling a certain way because it could have been triggered by something that happened earlier in her day.

Emotions are complicated. Often, the action and emotion we see on the surface is only a piece of what is really occurring underneath the visible emotional puzzle. This is referred to as the *emotion iceberg*. Just like a real iceberg, we can only see the tip of what is going on, and most of what is unfolding is hidden below the water.

For example, my daughter was yelling and seemingly angry with her brothers when she came home from school. We saw and heard the fury loud and

> **Just like a real iceberg, we can only see the tip of what is going on, and most of what is unfolding is hidden below the water.**

clear. What we did not see was the sadness and hurt she felt from a classmate getting in her face, saying no one wants to play with her, and encouraging the other fourth-grade girls in their circle not to interact with her. Initially, I did not dig down deeper to truly understand what was bothering her.

Since children are still growing and their brains are still developing, the emotion that initially comes out sometimes isn't even the emotion they truly feel. Children's brains can easily go into fight, flight, or freeze mode. Her body reacts this way when it perceives danger emotionally, mentally, or physically. For all of us, this can be caused by a stressful, frightening, or dangerous event, such as bullying. *Fight* is the body's response to protect itself. *Flight* means the body is telling the child to run from danger. *Freeze* is the body's inability to move or act against the perceived threat. When a child's immature brain goes into fight mode, its natural reaction is to get mad. This can manifest as yelling, stomping, slamming doors, throwing objects, hitting, punching, etc. This does not signify you have a mean child. This is just your child's brain sounding an alarm.

When a child is in this mode, you should not ask, "What is wrong with you?" or "Why are you angry?" When a child is in fight, flight, or freeze mode, she is not using the thinking part of her brain. The thinking brain is the part that makes logical decisions, reasons, and engages in conscious thoughts to express ideas through language. Your child is in her feeling brain when she is in fight, flight, or freeze mode. So you cannot ask questions or reason with your child at this moment.

What can you do? First, make sure your child is in a safe place, knows you love her, and understands you are there for her when she is ready to talk. Back off from her and give her space, but do not distance yourself from her unless she says, "Go away." If she asks you to go away, give her space but stay in eyesight of her. Let her calm down in whatever way is safest for her. Remember, she is not using her thinking brain, so now is not the time to tell her to take deep breaths, count down from ten, or try any calming technique unless she has practiced it several times before when she hasn't been in this mode.

Once she has calmed down, get curious! Be a detective and figure out where the emotion is coming from. Please do your child a favor and listen to her heart and head. If she is acting out at home, dig deeper, talk less, and listen more. Children's behavior sometimes speaks louder than the words they can share. Depending on the trauma or situation, know that this part may not get figured out as soon as you hope.

Dig deeper, talk less, and listen more.

The internal tornado.

A certified counselor shared with me that she refers to this emotional overload as an internal tornado. Picture a gingerbread person. Then picture a tornado of squiggly lines, drawn from icing, on the gingerbread's abdomen, shaped like a tornado. What can happen inside a child after a school day is a build-up of the emotions she felt throughout the day. If the child does not reach out to a trusted adult or if the adult doesn't listen intently, those emotions can swirl and swirl inside of the child. Since your home is your child's safest place, those emotions often come out there. When held inside for a longer period, they typically brew and then explode as anger. Sometimes, the child is truly angry. However, many times, it is another emotion that looks like anger, such as sadness, shame, frustration, embarrassment, anxiety, or others.

If your child hasn't bottled up too many emotions or events over time, you may be able to figure out what the deeper emotions and issues are by asking the right questions. The best questions to ask are questions that cannot be answered with a simple yes or no. Open-ended questions create the best results for problem-solving through this.

- What did you do at school today?
- Who did you play with?
- What did you do during recess?
- What specials did you go to?
- Who sat by you at lunch?
- What was your favorite thing about your day?
- What was the most challenging part of your day?

Then follow up with more questions to continue the conversation and advance your detective work. Make sure, though, that your child doesn't feel interrogated. You want to make this seem as organic as possible, truly showing her you are interested and care about her.

Depending on your child's vocabulary, maturity, and personality, questions may not be the most productive way to get the answers you seek. Another idea is to have your child draw or paint a picture of her day. You don't have to be an expert on this for it to be helpful. Sometimes, a simple color choice can tell you a lot about her day. If a child chooses red, she may be angry or embarrassed about something. Blue can represent sadness. Green—envy or jealousy. Purple can represent pride. Gray might reveal sadness or depression. Black could mean depression, extreme sadness, or uncertainty. Though, if a child is young, she may simply choose her favorite color. In that case, the color may not paint the picture you seek to uncover.

Overall, however, if a child likes to draw, a picture alone can speak volumes about how she feels.

The third option is to have your child journal. This is helpful for the child who likes to write about her day. This can be set up however best fits your child. One way is to have her write or draw daily and label what happened each day. Another way is to have her write in her journal whenever she has a strong feeling or event that she does not want to explain verbally. She may not want to say it out loud for many reasons, but a common one I have found in our home is she doesn't want her siblings to hear and know.

A fourth way is to have a two-way journal. This journal is one in which your child writes down a thought, event, or whatever else she wants to share with you. Then you read the entry and respond back in writing. This is especially helpful when a child has calmed down or it's a quiet time, such as naptime when she can't speak loudly, or at bedtime when those thoughts creep into her mind and she needs to get them out. There are other ways to use this resource, but these are four of the most common ways to journal to dig deeper.

Option number five is to reach out to your child's teacher. The best way to do this is through a phone call. If a phone call is not an option, then an email is the next best choice. You do not have to share everything that happened at home, but you can ask questions like, "Was there a change in the schedule today? Did you notice a different emotion in my child today? Did my child have a disagreement with another classmate? Did a situation happen today in the classroom/specials/lunchroom/playground that would make my child feel angry, sad, etc. (whatever emotion you think)? Did something embarrassing happen to my child? Do you have any ideas why my child would be _____ [state emotion]?" I was a teacher and can tell you a good teacher wants to help you and your child. However, if your child's teacher is not trustworthy or not the best resource, then do not use this option. It may do more harm.

Some children just need time to calm down and detach. If your child is not up for talking, just give her the space to decompress and come to you later. But make sure the door is left open in the room she is in and that she and her surroundings are kept safe. Every child has an internal clock and coping strategies that help her. Help her discover hers.

Every child is wired differently, and there is no one-size-fits-all method of soothing or healing. My daughter had been an open book until all of this happened—so much so that she would even tattle on herself! However, as you read in the Introduction, she was shutting me out about how her days at school were going. We will get into that in a later chapter, but for now, know we had to eventually seek professional help. You know your child best! Choose calming and communication strategies that fit her personality (and yours) to help her through this journey. If none of those resonate with you then get creative and do what works best for you and her.

> *We are now leaving home. Take a deep breath in and release a gentle breath out. Open the front door and hop in your vehicle of choice. We are headed to school. Remember, I am here with you, Mama. You are not in this alone.*

School Entrance Door

We have now arrived at school and are about to walk through the entrance. This is usually where new journeys start, joy and laughter fill the hallways and classrooms, friends hug, and children cannot wait to dive into a new book or learn a new game in PE. However, for your sweet child, this may not be the case. That is why we are here. Take a deep breath in and a deep breath out. This will pull at your heartstrings, but it is needed for the healing process for you and your child.

This is where *something* is going on. The school has become an *unsafe* zone for your child. Your child's body may even tense as she wakes up with the thought of passing through this entrance every morning. She may fight you to get ready and out the door of your home. If she's anything like my daughter was, then she may be sick to her stomach or have tears rolling down her face. Mama, this is not how school is supposed to be! Now, don't get me wrong; school has its challenging moments, but it should not produce a horrible mind game that your child has to play day in and day out. Stay with me as we get curious about what is really going on.

Bullying happens in all shapes and forms. It knows no boundaries when it comes to gender, race, personality, ethnicity, socioeconomic status, or IQ level. No school is exempt. It happens in public, private, magnet, academy, charter, secular, and parochial schools. As long as free will exists, bullying will happen. In 2023, nearly one out of five students reported being bullied. That is almost 20 percent of students! In the South, in 2023, that was over 8.5 million students ages twelve to eighteen[1]. And that stat only reflects the students who shared they had been bullied. Research and my professional and personal experience show there are even more students who are not divulging to anyone they have been bullied, especially students who are scared of repercussions or revenge brought upon them by the child who is bullying if that information is disclosed. I am not condoning this at all; I am merely bringing to light the nature of the beast. Know my professional and mama heart here. I have taught for more than fourteen years now and have been a strong advocate for stopping this problem in its tracks.

Before we discuss the forms of bullying, we need to define what bullying is and what it is not. As Dr. Sally Kuykendall says, "Bullying is when one or more persons with power repeatedly abuse a person with lesser power for the purpose of causing harm, distress, or fear."[2] To be considered bullying, the act must contain the following:

1. Purposeful action.
2. Malicious intent (hurt, embarrassment, humiliation, or intimidation).
3. Repetition (but it doesn't always have to be the same action).
4. Imbalance of power between the victim and bully, where the bully has greater power.

Bullying needs to meet all four of the above criteria. Because of this, we must make a distinction between "rude behavior," "mean behavior," and "bullying." Not all rude behavior is bullying. Best-selling author Signe Whitson defines rude as "inadvertently saying or doing something that hurts someone else."[3] Some examples of children being rude are a boy laughing when a peer drops the football instead of catching it, saying a girl's hairdo is ugly, throwing mud at a boy's face, or pointing out that a child wore the same shirt the day before. Rude behavior happens once and is spontaneous, said thoughtlessly, borne from poor manners, and not purposely meant to hurt someone.

Mean behavior on the other hand is "purposely saying or doing something to hurt someone once (or maybe twice)."[4] The main difference between rude and mean behavior is rude behavior is unintentional, whereas mean behavior is purposeful. Examples of mean behavior are criticizing the clothing another child wears; saying another child is fat or negatively commenting on another child's appearance; calling a peer "dumb," "stupid," or another similar word; telling another classmate another peer is "not cool," or anything else that purposely puts down the child being talked about.

Meanness can cause pain and wound the target, but it differs from bullying. One main difference between meanness and bullying is the intent. Typically, a child choosing to be mean is not intentionally choosing to harm a peer or show intentional aggressive behavior like a child who is bullying. Additionally, the meanness is not repeated over time, especially when an adult intervenes and stops the behavior from continuing. Third, the exchange is not happening between two peers with an imbalance of power or position. Therefore, the intervention taken by adults to counter the meanness is different from the intervention taken when someone is choosing to bully. However, if the meanness happens more than once to the same child, then it has shifted to bullying behavior. Overall, bullying comprises these three key elements, where meanness does not: intent to harm, repeated acts over time, and a power imbalance.

Now that we have discussed the differences between rude, mean, and bullying behavior, we can unpack the four broad forms of bullying. The first is the most detected in schools. This is *physical bullying*. Antibullyingsoftware.com gives the best definition for this type of bullying. "Physical bullying is using one's body and physical bodily acts to exert power over peers. Punching, kicking and other physical attacks are all types of physical bullying."[5] Physical bullying can be a simple poke in the belly or a powerful punch in the face that lands the victim on the ground, bleeding and bruised—or anything in between. In addition to the common types of physical bullying, depriving a peer of her personal belongings, stealing a peer's item, failing to return an item, intentionally damaging belongings, or manipulating a peer to give him a gift are also forms of physical bullying. The effects of physical bullying are easier for a parent or teacher to recognize because there is some kind of injured body part or a missing or broken personal belonging. Often, a mark, bruise, blood, or other bodily effect is left on the child.

If your child is or has experienced physical bullying, hopefully, she has made you aware. When physical bullying happens, take a picture of the area as long as it is not in the private area. Try to write down the entire story to have documentation of the situation. This does not have to be a cumbersome task, but it is much needed to keep your child safe. Documenting it will also help your child not have to retell the story over and over, as that adds to the trauma. Report it to the school authorities right away. If the school is closed for the day, at least email an administrator and then follow up the next morning with a phone call if they do not reach out to you first. Every state and school has its own rules and policies on how to report physical bullying and the next steps to take. We will get into more of that later; right now, we are problem-solving to understand what exactly is happening.

There are instances when physical bullying does not leave a lasting mark. When this happens, by the time your child gets home, the evidence of physical bullying cannot be seen on the outside. This was the case for my child. My fourth-grade daughter was in PE class, playing a game of tag. If a student was tagged, they had to go off the court and form a line of those who were "out." Madison got out, and her rule-following personality took her to the line. The child who was bullying got out next and was mad about it. Instead of going to the back of the line, as the teacher had instructed, she started at the front and quickly ran down the line, slapping students who were already lined up. My daughter was one of the children slapped.

Another instance happened to her on the playground. She was happily playing tag with a group of girls. As she climbed up the playset stairs to chase her peers, the child who was bullying blocked the opening at the top with her body. Madison looked at the child and kindly said, "Move out of my way."

The child who was bullying replied, "Say please."

Madison acquiesced and said, "Please move out of my way." She walked up the rest of the stairs, and as she entered the landing area, the child who was bullying stomped on her foot. My daughter, in self-defense, pushed the child who was bullying to get her off of her foot so she could run after the other girls and tag them. The child who was bullying turned around and with all her might tried to shove my daughter off the playset, which was high off the ground. Thankfully, Madison had faster reflexes and barely got out of the reach of the child who was bullying, or we would have had a more physically harmful outcome. In both of these physical bullying instances, there were no marks left behind for me to capture on camera. However, Madison's foot was sore, and she walked with a slight limp for a day or two. That was when I got curious and asked questions to figure out what happened.

Verbal or nonverbal bullying is the second form of bullying. Sometimes this bullying happens by itself, while other times, it happens in conjunction with physical bullying. Verbal bullying consists of insults, taunts, name-calling, cruel gossip, and other spoken language used to hurt a child verbally. This type can start less severely—more like simple teasing—but it can quickly escalate to physical bullying. My daughter experienced varying forms of verbal bullying. A bullying situation with less severity happened on the playground. My daughter was with a group of classmates. They were deciding what to play next when one of the girls looked at the group and said, "We don't want Madison to play with us, right?" As an isolated event, this was a mean gesture. However, this continued for a month. The child who was bullying made sure to let Madison initially walk with them, but then after they chose what they were going to do, the child who was bullying verbally explained why the other girls should not include her. A more severe example from my daughter's experience was when the child who was bullying sauntered up to my daughter's face, leaving only inches between them. Then the child who was bullying called her a name and boldly hurled other mean words at her.

Nonverbal bullying also pairs with verbal bullying. However, nonverbal bullying is harder to detect as most bullies do this when authorities are not looking. Common forms of nonverbal bullying are eye-rolling, nasty looks, obscene gestures, expressions of dislike or put-downs, and messages sent through letters, notes, or electronic devices.

The child who is bullying is sneaky if they are verbally abusing a student. They may whisper or wait until they are in a spot where an adult cannot hear them, such as in the bathroom, on the playground, or in the hall. If it is not an isolated incident, the targeted child's self-worth gets stripped away with every recurring incident. The child being bullied loses her sense of power over her life. She begins to believe the words spoken over and at her, and she believes she is less than who she really is. Our daughter felt all of this when she was in the thick of it! Just like we experienced, the child doesn't always speak up and instead internalizes it. By hiding what is going on, her parent has a difficult time even knowing this type of bullying is happening.

The most common way it is revealed is through a change in the child's behavior. For example, our daughter was a smiley, happy girl before she was bullied. As the bullying continued, she became downcast and eventually angry, exhibiting outbursts and sometimes even physically hurting her brothers, whom she dearly loved.

Psychological bullying is the third type and presents as "actions that are intended to result in embarrassment, humiliation, indignity, grief, or emotional upset."[6] Common forms of psychological bullying are mocking, sarcasm, belittling, ignoring, excluding from a group, lying, humiliating, spreading nasty rumors, depriving a peer of needed resources so that person has to ask or beg for assistance, threatening to hurt someone, forcing someone to do something against her free will, getting a peer in trouble by purposely exaggerating a minor offense or providing false information, or ganging up on others. Psychological bullying tends to be very sneaky and easily missed by the professionals in the school. However, it is also very intentional. The child who is bullying is underhanded in her tactics because she tries to hide it from the adult who is present. However, she is manipulating and controlling her victim. She has every intention of making the bullied student feel less than—not worthy enough.

This bullying happens because the child who is doing the bullying wants to feel like she has control. She hopes to dominate her situation and others and make herself look like the best option for her peers as they compare her to the person she is tearing down. She feels like if she uses her control and power to take down the one she is bullying, peers will see her as strong, and possibly even fear her. There are countless reasons why this form of bullying takes place. Some of the common reasons include:

- The child who is bullying mimics the behavior she sees in her home.
- Her home life is out of control, and she strives to maintain control at school.
- Jealousy of a personality trait in the one she is bullying.
- Experiencing mental turmoil that makes her angry so she chooses a peer who seems weaker to take out her anger on.

- Not wanting to share a friend so she tries to make the other peer look less desirable.
- And the list goes on and on . . .

To better understand psychological bullying, we are going to look at two ways my daughter experienced this type. The first scenario happened in the classroom. The entire fourth-grade class was seated at their desks, completing independent work. Madison was focusing on her paper when she felt a tap. She turned, and a classmate passed her a note, saying it was from her best friend. Madison smiled, turned around, and quickly unfolded the note. This note did not contain the happy words she expected. Instead, it read something like, "You are not being a nice friend. I do not want to play with you anymore because you are mean." It felt like her heart was torn in two. She thought, *How could my best friend think that?*

When I picked her up from school, a dark cloud hovered over her. Her face was downcast, and she was not her bubbly self. She rode home quietly. Once we all piled out of the van and into our house, I took her aside and was able to get the story out of her. With tears rolling down her face, she explained the hurt her friend had caused. She didn't understand why her friend would even write that at all, let alone to her. She voiced that she tried to be really nice and include everyone, as long as they were being kind. She felt sick to her stomach, and she feared going to that friend's upcoming party because "Mom, she won't want me there. She thinks I'm mean. What if the other girls team up against me and are mean to me too?"

As her mom, it broke my heart that she was going through all this emotional and mental pain. I did what I thought was best, and I reached out to her friend's mom. I told her what happened and that Madison no longer felt comfortable attending her friend's birthday party. This mama assured me that she would talk to her daughter—that she would try to get to the bottom of what happened. Our two girls were good friends, and she did not believe her daughter would make this hurtful gesture.

Minutes later my phone buzzed with a text from the friend's mom. Sure enough, the passed note was not kept in its original form. The classmate who had passed the note to Madison had added mean words to the note before handing it off to her. By then, the hurt had already happened, my daughter felt emotionally drained, and she no longer looked forward to the birthday party. The child who was bullying got what she wanted: my daughter felt lesser than and the child who was bullying did not have to share their mutual friend.

Example two took place on the playground. The same child bullying Madison in scenario one was playing a game at recess with Madison and a small group of classmates. Madison was supposed to count while the other girls hid, and then she was tasked with finding them after counting. Madison ran away to count, as planned. While she galloped away, the child who was bullying whispered to the circle of girls not to play with my daughter and to instead run away and do something else. One of the girls in the circle spoke up and said, "No, Amanda [fake name used for confidentiality], I want to play with Madison. You are being mean." That friend then walked over to my daughter to tell her what happened, and they played together for the rest of the recess. My daughter felt sad that the child who was bullying had tried to plan something hurtful, but she was grateful her friend stood up for her and chose to play with her.

The newest, most advanced, and potentially most dangerous form of bullying is cyberbullying. Cyberbullying is the use of electronic communication to bully a person. As author Dr. Joel Haber states in *Bully Proof Your Child for Life*, "The internet is the new bathroom wall."[7] Unlike other forms of bullying, cyberbullying follows the child wherever she goes, through texts, gaming, and social networks and apps, all right on her phone. This means a child can be bullied online and offline at the same time.

Cyberbullying can take on six basic forms.

1. Direct bullying.

    Direct bullying is when the child who is bullying expresses hurtful, vulgar, offensive, or threatening language to hurt the person receiving the messages through email, text messages, or messenger apps. An example is a female high schooler texting a peer: "Sally, what were you wearing today? Did you even look in the mirror? Girl, you are the worst-dressed person in high school. Why do you even come to school anymore?" The intention is to offend the target and make her feel "less than" or "lower than" the one sending the message.

2. Impersonation.

    One student impersonates another student and sends messages saying they are from the victim. These messages contain false gossip, secretive information, embarrassing information about the victim or someone else, or information that makes authorities think the victim is bullying someone else even though it was another person writing the message. For example, a middle school girl sends a text to a boy saying, "Hey, John, this is Anna. You were looking fine today. Let's meet up today at _____." It looks like the text was from Anna, but really, Zoe sent it to John, pretending to be Anna. Anna has no idea about this text, and John shows up at the place Anna had told her friends she was going to be.

3. Posting embarrassing, hurtful, or hate-filled photos or videos.

    The child who is bullying posts embarrassing videos others have made, have gotten ahold of, or have created themselves of the "target" on platforms, such as YouTube. Students often record videos or take a series of photos of the target on their phones and then post online directly, creating reels, or YouTube videos, with the photos or video footage. Some examples of where these videos are taken are on the bus, in the locker room, in the bathroom, at a party, at a gathering, or even in school if phone use is not closely monitored. The photos or videos can be enhanced with photo-editing programs or video apps. The intention is to embarrass, gossip about, or make the bullied student feel small, or lesser than the child who is doing the bullying. The child who is bullying is degrading the other child to take power away from her.

4. Gossip groups.
Private groups view images or posts online, via email, or in a chain of messages among several children as a text message or in a messenger app. This is where students come together and discuss kids they don't like, bash peers, or even vote for the "most hated student," "ugliest student," "dumbest student," and more. The comments are online for anyone to read and, if not deleted, can remain online forever, serving as a constant reminder and point of pain for the target.

5. Harassing websites.
It is simple to create a new website, and some providers offer them for free. In the short time since the World Wide Web was born, children have learned how to design websites dedicated to harassing peers. In his book, Dr. Joel Haber shares about one such website, "Kill Kylie Incorporated."[8] The purpose of this website was to accuse a girl of being gay and threaten her life online. He goes on to report it took nine months for the police to find the bullies behind this website because of how easy it is to hide your identity.

This may shock you as a parent—as it did me at first. However, I was reminded of how easily people steal our identities on platforms like Facebook and Instagram, and even through financial platforms and store apps. Websites are no different in that they are easily formed and can be used for negative purposes too.

6. Unwanted email registrations and subscriptions.
   This is where a child who is bullying signs up the victim for ongoing memberships or subscriptions by pretending to be them. The child who is bullying only needs the other child's name and email to accomplish this. Then he can register the target for unwanted emails, such as inappropriate blogs, teen magazines created for the opposite gender, sexual newsletters, porn, gay propaganda, and anything else that would embarrass, offend, or annoy the child on the receiving end. This child who is bullying can go as far as registering them for things that would alert parents and school authorities, having them falsely believe these students are trying to harm themselves, their peers, or the school.

Cyberbullying is a sneaky form of bullying that makes it difficult to trace who is behind the actions. The child who is bullying is shielded by perceptions of invisibility. The child who is bullying anonymously hides behind a screen, which limits retaliation by the victim since the child tends not to know who is behind it. It's also hard for adults, school authorities, and police to detect the instigator who has access to the target online and offline. Therefore, it has become one of the severest forms of nonverbal bullying.

All forms of bullying are hurtful and unacceptable—and should be addressed in school. As the form(s) of how your child is being bullied surfaces, please keep written, documentation to track the facts your child shares with you. This will not only help you have clear specifics on what to share with your child's teacher and school personnel, but it will also help your child avoid repeatedly living through the trauma by having to retell the story. Write down the date(s), where it happened, what happened, and how it impacted your child. Then reach out to the school. If the teacher is a respected and trusted adult, then I challenge you to first contact the teacher. A video call or in-person meeting are the best options. That way, you can see each other, and the teacher can better understand and hear the emotions and nonverbals you exhibit as you share the facts. Sometimes, because of schedules or time of day, the next best option is phone, then email. A benefit of an email is that it keeps a "paper trail" if you need it in the future.

There are instances when a teacher is not a safe person or a good advocate for your child. As a former teacher and fellow mama, I know and have witnessed this to be true. I want to make you aware of that and give you permission to move up the professional ladder if needed. As long as the principal is an advocate for your child and family, reach out to that person.

Once again, a face-to-face meeting for the first time you share this type of factual information is the most ideal. Call the principal and give a synopsis of what is going on, making sure to express the urgency of the meeting. He needs to know that your child is not safe and that you desire to work together to eliminate the bullying. At the meeting, share the date(s) of when it happened, where it happened, how it happened, and how your child was impacted. Then the principal can explain the proper procedures for what must be followed, and together, you can make a plan for how to help your child feel comfortable at school and ensure the bullying ceases, or harsher action will be taken. Your overall goal is to help your child feel safe again and not fear going to school.

We are now leaving school. Take a deep breath in and a gentle breath out. Shake the dust off your feet—the hurt you just had to share. I am proud of you. You just took one of the hardest steps in this journey. You advocated for your child. Well done, Mama! Many parents do not take this big step because of peer pressure or worry about what others will think of them. I am so very proud of you. The difficult work is not done yet, though. Slide into your driver's seat. We are headed home again. However, once we arrive, we will enter a dark room that most parents do not get to enter. It is the attic—into our child's mind. Please remember, I am here with you, Mama. You are not alone in this next step.

The Attic
Into the Child's Mind

We have now crawled through the trap door, and we are in the child's mind. Just like in the movie *Inside Out*, you will experience many emotions here. One minute, you will be experiencing fear, then in the next minute, anger then anxiety, shame, exhaustion . . . and the list will go on and on. Please remember, this is a delicate space, so tiptoe as you go along, and do not touch anything right now. Just observe and try to understand what is going on, but do not attempt to fix anything. Your job is to be an observer, a detective, while you are here. Some things you see in this room have been kept secret for many reasons. As you try to understand things from your child's perspective, take it all in but know you are not the mechanic right now. We will "fix"—or better yet, "restore"—broken areas later, in another room. As you gaze into all of these areas, your own feelings may spike; this may even bring up past trauma for you. Make note of that and be gentle with yourself too.

As you tiptoe into the child's mind, you might feel taken out at your knees by the swirling exclamatory sentences. You duck to save your footing, but you can't help but notice the bright, bold, red words that keep coming at you. It's as if they are on fire. *No one likes me! Everyone hates me! I am the worst. No one wants to be my friend. No one will play with me. I'm the worst person in the world! I wish I wasn't alive!* This is *anger*. Your child is angry with how she is being treated at school. She is shaming herself because of all the untruths the child who is bullying her is saying. Internally, your sweet child has lost her innocence. The child who is bullying is robbing her of the truths you've helped to lay as a foundation, and that person has filled her head with toxic lies. She is struggling to see her worth and identity because she is being torn down emotionally, mentally, or even physically.

Kids *are not resilient*! Instead, just like adults, kids *are human*. Children have breaking points. This precious child has hit her breaking point head-on! Her head is being filled with negative thoughts and false "I am" statements.

As you trek, all of the red disappears, and now the room is bathed in ultraviolet light. Ideas are flying all over the place, like a whirlwind, but they are not landing. Instead, they are colliding as they fly around. This is *shame. I am dumb. I am ugly. I am unlovable. I am unseen. I am weak. I am useless. I am unlikable.* As this internal monologue swirls, a big, bold warning sign brightens the room. "Just don't share anything! Don't tell anyone what's happening! No one will believe you!" A whisper comes across: *Shh, keep this to yourself this is not safe to share. You are the reason this is happening. Even your parents won't believe you. Keep this to yourself.*

In her mind, you can see her looking at her brothers. The purple hue in her mind turns to red again. One of her brothers runs down the hall with her favorite toy. Anger is back. *Ahhh, no one likes me! He is so mean! Why can't he just leave me alone?*

"Stomp down the hall!!! Push him over!" the red chants loudly. "He doesn't like you. He is the worst." She agrees with the whispered lies. *He always takes my things.*

As she grabs the toy, you hear her yell, "Why can't you just leave me alone? You are the worst! Don't take my things!" As the words are hurled from her mouth, she shoves her brother.

In full focus, you see a picture of yourself pop up. You look mad and frustrated, and you are talking to your child about what just happened. The red turns back to ultraviolet because of the relentless cycle between shame and anger. *I am dumb. I am unlovable. I am unseen.* The big, bold warning sign flashes again. *Just don't share! Don't tell anyone what is going on. No one will believe you! You are the reason this is happening.*

A blue-gray hue now engulfs the room. It is a thick haze that takes over. This is *sadness*. Images start flashing through her mind. Today's bullying experience is taking over her thoughts. Flashback feelings of her pain and sadness exist on replay. The mean words leave wounds in her mind, like scratches on her brain. The emotional bullying is playing Tug of War with her emotions. The physical wound aches. Questions saunter through her mind: *Why is she so mean to me? Why does she hate me? Why won't she leave me alone? Why me?* Then the flood comes; the tears cannot stop falling.

The room immediately shifts to a dark gray color. She has buried herself in a pillow, and her mind is almost numb. It does not know what direction to go now. What to think at all. Her mind is tired of going back and forth. In the distance, a quiet voice enters: "Time to eat. Dinner is ready." The gray lingers, and the words fall to the ground. She is feeling *detachment* from the present and from her emotions. Food sounds gross, unappetizing.

Thankfully, this time, the room lightens to a brighter gray. With the bit of energy she has left, she mouths the words, *I am not hungry.* Then the room fades off into a dark gray cloud once again.

After what seems like hours (but is only minutes), the room lightens again. Images of her family fill the room. They appear to be eating dinner. You see her plate float into the room. All of the food is blurry. She is still feeling detached. Parts of phrases blow through the room, but they are jumbled. Her family is speaking to her, but she does not understand anything they say. She is numb, not present.

The room turns eerily black. Fearful dreams are flashing throughout the room. The child who is bullying is shoving her down. Insults pierce her side. Friends walk away from her on the playground. She is alone on the swings. No one is in sight. The recess teacher points a finger at her. "This is all your fault! You bring this on yourself!"

A bright orange light shines through the room. Your eyes burn. This is *anxiety*. Nightmares flash through the room once more, and she is anxious about the next day at school. The room has a clashing sound ringing through it. This is all the noise that fills her head as she frets about the what-ifs that may happen in the upcoming day. *She's going to be mean again! She's going to make me feel bad. My friends are not going to play with me. I am going to be all alone.* A loud heartbeat blares in the room. It is her racing heart as she thinks of the unknowns and worries about the nightmares becoming real.

A mirrored reflection shines into the room; it is her image in the mirror. She has cuts and bruises. Those are the hurts the child who is bullying or children who are bullying have placed in her mind and possibly on her body. Her face is downcast, tear-stained, and scarred. She looks for hope in the shadow of the mirror. That is you! She is looking for your hand and a piece of your heart to help her get through.

> *The reflection hits you, and you see a small light guiding you back to the trap door. You gently wade through the noise, plugging your ears as they ring. Tiptoe as you follow the light. You are leaving the child's mind. You are crawling back through the trap door and landing in the Living Room.*

Living Room Door

Let's walk through the Living Room Door. Deep breath in. Loud, deep breath out. Repeat as many times as needed. This is your safety zone. You can let down your guard and experience all the feelings as you process your day. You might cry. You might yell. I give you permission to scream if it helps you release what you have bottled up inside. You have tried to save face and stay calm amid all the turmoil and chaos. The good news is problems will be solved in this room. This is where the "rubber will hit the road."

We just left the most difficult room—the attic. You saw many emotions and "experienced" much of your child's struggle there. Did the emotions surprise you as they showed up? Let's unpack it all here, where you are free to be you—feelings and all.

Before we start, I recommend grabbing a notebook and pen. As you ponder, take note of what you learn, what you notice about your child, what questions you still have, the things you don't understand, and anything that arises that you do not want to forget.

There are several behaviors a child being bullied can show on the outside. Some behaviors are easy to see while others are easy to miss. Be a detective, and look closely at which ones your child displays. Below is a list of the most common behaviors exhibited. We will unpack them in more detail.

- Intense emotional responses.
- Mean words said about self or others.
- Avoiding sharing about her school day.

- Loss of appetite.
- Crying and not wanting to get up in the morning.
- Waking up in the middle of the night and struggling to go back to sleep.
- Lack of motivation to play.
- Detaching from or avoiding enjoyable activities.
- Avoiding homework.
- Being forgetful.
- Ignoring daily chores.
- Not completing simple tasks.

Intense Emotional Responses

This behavior is the easiest one to spot. Your daughter can go from sad to angry in a matter of seconds. As discussed previously, emotions are complicated. Often, the emotional responses we see on the surface are only a piece of what is occurring underneath those reactions. Recall that this is referred to as the *emotion iceberg*. Just like a real iceberg, we can only see the tip of what is going on, but most of what is happening is hidden below the water. Since children are still growing and their brains are still developing, so the emotion that initially comes out isn't always the emotion they feel.

While your child was at school, she may have bottled up all the emotions she felt, especially when around the child who bullied her. Remember the gingerbread girl image we discussed in "Home Front Door?" Inside the gingerbread girl's stomach is a tornado of squiggly lines. If the child did not reach out to a trusted adult or if the adult didn't listen intently, those emotions continue to swirl inside the child. Since the home is your child's safest place, those emotions will eventually come out there. When held inside for a long period, they brew and explode as anger.

Anger was the red hue in the child's mind in the attic you visited. This color showed up when she thought about the events of her day when the child who was bullying made her feel *less than*. This is when she has negative thoughts about herself, such as, "Everyone hates me!" Anger also shows up when she gets frustrated at home. What used to produce a slight irritation can now feel like an all-out war. Her emotions have been on a roller-coaster ride for too long, and she can no longer regulate simple irritants.

Sometimes anger comes out when she is feeling another emotion. This goes back to the phenomenon of fight, flight, or freeze. When a child's immature brain goes into fight mode, a natural reaction is to get angry. This can look like yelling, stomping, slamming doors, throwing objects, hitting, punching, slapping, or _____ (fill in the blank for your child). Fight mode looks different from child to child. Your child is not a mean child. This is just the brain's outward representation of believing there is danger emotionally, mentally, or physically.

Mean Words

When your daughter is angry, she can blurt out mean words about herself or others. Common ones about herself are "No one likes me," "Everyone hates me!" and "I'm the worst person in the world!" or "I wish I wasn't alive!" Each of these sentences carries a message that her immature brain is struggling to verbalize.

No one likes me. Everyone hates me! These two go hand-in-hand. They are attached to one or more stories where she felt left out. This could be in a classroom, during PE, at recess, at lunch, or during a sport or game. Was she not chosen by the teacher for a classroom job? Did a classmate not choose her as a partner for a project? Was she the last one to get assigned something? During PE, was she rejected by the "good" team or a captain? Did everyone try to get her out during tag? Did the bullying child whisper mean statements about her? Did the child who is bullying tell lies about her to her peers? Did classmates point at her and snicker? During recess, did other girls exclude her from their play? Did the child who is bullying tell her no one likes her? Did a peer say don't pick _____ [your child's name]?

I am the worst! This statement can carry multiple meanings. One comes from a child who is bullying her by continually pointing out something about your child. For example, the bullying child might say, "Look at how ugly Sarah's hair is." This does not necessarily hold true, but if the child who is bullying says it repeatedly, Sarah can internalize it as truth.

I wish I wasn't alive! This statement should wave a big red flag in your face. It means your child has reached her breaking point. Her head has been filled with negative thoughts and destructive "I am" statements. She is angry with how she is treated at school, and she is done dealing with it. She is shaming herself with all the untruths the child who is bullying spouts to her, perhaps daily. Internally, this sweet child has lost her innocence. The child who is bullying is robbing her of truth by filling her head with toxic lies. She is struggling to see her worth and identity because she is being torn down emotionally, mentally, or even physically.

Your child is waving her "I surrender" flag. This means your child needs your intervention—and probably a professional to help her navigate everything she has bottled up, especially mentally. If you can find a calm time, ask open-ended questions to encourage her to elaborate on why she said she shouldn't be alive. Though, like others who have taken so many emotional and mental beatings, she may not know why she feels this way. She just knows she thinks the world would be better off without her. If that is the case, I highly recommend you reach out to a counselor and make an appointment. Depending on your child's age, this could be very serious, and your child might be battling depression and suicidal thoughts. If that is the case, I highly recommend calling the suicide hotline in your state or reaching out to a Christian counselor to see if you can get in ASAP. If you cannot get into a counselor quickly, you may want to contact your child's doctor to find out what the doctor recommends as the next best step for your child.

Avoiding Sharing about Her School Day

Being consistently vague about the school day might show up when children who used to share the events of their day are dealing with bullying. I am talking about the girl who, the instant you picked her up from school, used to rattle off the good and the bad, from the beginning of her school day to the end. Or this is the child who, when you asked, "How was your day?" had no problem listing her favorite parts, from recess to lunch conversations to the book she read.

Now, when you ask how her day went, she replies with a shrug or pretends she didn't hear you. Let's go back into "The Attic," where we saw what was going on in her mind, to dive deeper. In that space, this is when the room turned ultraviolet. Remember? Ideas flew everywhere, like a whirlwind, but they did not land anywhere concrete or stable. Instead, they collided as they flew around. That was the feeling of *shame*. Her head was filled with negative thoughts and unhealthy "I am" statements like, "I am dumb." Or I am ugly. I am unlovable. I am unseen. I am weak. I am useless. I am unlikable.

Then the warning sign lit up the room with the bright words, "Just don't share! Don't tell anyone what's going on! No one will believe you!" A whisper came across: *Shh, keep this to yourself; this is not safe to share. You are the reason this is happening. Even your parents won't believe you. Keep this to yourself.*

She has believed all of those lies, and she is obeying that danger sign created inside her head. She believes it is her fault, so she doesn't want anyone to know, to risk exposing her faults or weaknesses. If you are a Christian believer, you understand this is the enemy, trying to steal Truth and destroy her true identity and worth. If he can shame her, then she is trapped, and that is exactly where he wants her to stay.

You must be a detective again and figure out what she is *not* sharing. Remember, she is feeling shame right now so tread lightly. You may have to get creative. Ask open-ended questions you do not normally ask. Play worship music. Or go back to the "Home Front Door" chapter and try one or more of the tips listed there.

If none of these get to the bottom of what is going on, I suggest seeking a good professional counselor. There is no shame in asking for help for your child—or for yourself. We needed a Christian counselor for our daughter. The "Living Room Door" chapter will help you choose a counselor who fits your personality and family situation. In addition, the "Counselor's Office Door" will also reveal the value our family gained from counseling.

Loss of Appetite

Most children feel hungry at certain parts of the day. They wake up hungry in the morning; after school, they rush to the kitchen for an afternoon snack, and dinner cannot come fast enough. Can you relate? However, when a child is being bullied, food doesn't sound good. When you are sick and feeling miserable, the last thing you want to be around is a strong-smelling meal. This is the same symptom of bullying after it has consumed your child's energy every day and feelings of defeat have seeped into her mind. She has no appetite because there is no room inside for food. Her mind, body, and soul are *full* from the all-consuming battering.

This might start simply. Perhaps she skips her daily after-school snack. You may brush it off and think she had a big lunch and still feels full. Or maybe she is coming down with something and is not feeling well. However, it is when she says she's not hungry and brushes off bigger meals that your ears should perk up and you think, *Something is not right here!*

Think back to "The Attic" (flip back for reference if that helps). Her mind is tired of all the thinking and going back and forth with her emotions and the various scenarios. In a short time, she can go from sadness to anger and then to despair. If you will recall, *shame* enters the room. And shame is a monster! It overtakes everything and is so hard to shake. When your beautiful child is thick in the shame arena, she will believe she is not worth anything—not even worthy of eating. She may wonder what the point is. *I am useless, ugly, fat, horrible*—insert the false truths the child who is bullying has spoken over her. These emotions can overtake her entire body and trick her into thinking she is not hungry at all. In reality, she may not have eaten all day, and her body is craving food.

Stress affects the entire body. When we are stressed, certain hormones are triggered. It can set our bodies into that fight or flight mode, and it can trick us into thinking we are in danger. Our children's bodies are no different. Her entire body is affected when she is emotionally overloaded and stressed. Her body, just like ours, starts sending defense mechanisms, and certain natural processes and systems are put into motion, set on protecting her from any danger.

One or two missed meals will not harm your child. She will feel weaker, but she will be okay. As you uncover why she is not eating, make it a goal to get her to eat again. However, when she makes it a habit of not ever eating or starts losing weight, that is when you need to seek professional help. It does not mean you are a bad parent. It means this is bigger than you and her, and she needs a professional trained in trauma and counseling practices to provide the necessary aid. That counselor can dig deeper, get to the root cause, and help her find her worth again—even if just to help her fuel her body with food.

Crying and Not Wanting to Get Up in the Morning

Some children love going to school; some children do not. The behavior of not wanting to get up in the morning can be a sign that your child is being bullied. For a child who is not a morning person, this behavior becomes heightened. For example, Suzy is not naturally a morning person. She takes more coaxing to get up. However, when she is being bullied, instead of going back to sleep or pulling the covers over her head, she cries when you tell her to get up. She yells at you once you wake her up. She normally does not like to get up in the morning, but now her behavior is more extreme and may be coupled with verbal or even physical sadness or anger, or both.

No child should shed a tear when she realizes it is a school day. There are exceptions, such as when she is sick, it is the last day of school and she doesn't want it to end, someone has died, someone has moved, or another big transition is happening in her life. For the most part, though, there is no reason why a child should cry over going to school.

For the child who is by nature a morning person, this behavior of not wanting to get up and experiencing intense sadness or anger in the morning should be a red flag. She might be fearful of going to school because she doesn't know what lies ahead after she passes through the school's doors. Her mind spirals as daylight hits her eyes, and she does not want to begin a day filled with unknowns or threats. *Will he hit me? Will she call me names today? Will he make me cry at recess in front of all my friends?* These questions and whatever negative behavior she is enduring at school will be swirling around in her head from the moment her eyes open in the morning to the moment she closes them and falls asleep. She will fear all of those possibilities, and she may even ruminate on the worst-case scenarios before her feet hit the floor.

You do not want to diminish or downplay the feelings she is experiencing. First, be aware that you cannot rush this process. Don't hurry her through her morning routine and get her off to school. Instead, be okay with the idea of her being late—or not going to school at all that day. Second, if you do not know everything going on, dig deep with probing questions to understand where the fears are coming from and why she is wrestling with them. Next, help her name those fears, and then you can validate them. Help her understand who the safe people are at her school so she can identify the allies to help her if any scenarios begin to play out.

After you get to the root cause of the fears, help her believe what is true. Have her repeat confidence-building "I am" statements about her that are true. For example, instead of "You are so stupid," which the child who is bullying might be saying to her, flip it to "I am smart." Don't stop there. Share Scripture with her that speaks the same truth of the "I am" statement over her. We will unpack more of this exercise in the chapter called, "The Child's Bathroom."

Once she starts to calm down and believe the truth enough to get ready for school, you should tell her how proud you are of her for sharing this with you. Let her know you are always willing and wanting to talk to her when she needs to talk. Tell her nothing is too small or too big to share. You are an open ear for her and willing to listen and not talk if that's what she prefers. Also, share how everything that has happened to her is not her fault. It is not a reflection of who she is. Tell her that you are going to do everything in your power to stop the bullying and that you never want her to feel unsafe at school.

There is no magic timeframe for how soon a child will open up, but you are the parent. You know when enough is enough and your sweet child needs a professional to help them. Please know from the bottom of my mama heart that you are not a failure for needing professional help. Initially, I felt shame in seeking help. However, I quickly learned that when a child has a fever and certain other symptoms of distress, a parent takes her to the doctor to get help. When a child has a painful tooth, a parent takes her to the dentist. When a child has an open wound that won't stop bleeding, her parent rushes her to the hospital. Seeking out a counselor should be no different. Mental health is just as crucial as physical health. Professional support can make all the difference for a child emotionally, mentally, and physically.

Waking Up in the Middle of the Night and Struggling to Go Back to Sleep

There are certain stages and ages when children wake up in the middle of the night after experiencing bad dreams or night terrors. Sometimes this is because of what happened the previous day, what they watched on an electronic device, a subconscious thought that went unresolved before going to sleep, or something else. The list could go on. Other times, waking up happens when their brains are developing at certain stages, and other times, night terrors just happen.

This behavior alone shouldn't make you immediately think your child is being bullied. However, if any of the other behaviors are revealing themselves through your child in conjunction with nightmares, you should make note of this and dig deeper.

With our daughter, she would wake up in the middle of the night either sobbing, yelling, "Mom!" or both. Before she shared with me what was happening at school, I thought she was just experiencing bad dreams. Once she opened up, I learned her mind was either replaying what had happened the previous day or, worse, her mind had dreamed up a horrible nightmare of the worst-case scenario that she feared might happen the next day at school.

When this behavior becomes a pattern, the child wakes up exhausted for the day ahead. Thus, her learning is impacted because she cannot focus or concentrate. Also, her short-term and long-term memory will be impacted because her brain isn't refreshed and cannot work properly without adequate, sound sleep. Her growth can also be affected since, according to research, the human body grows the most while a child sleeps. So not getting a good night's sleep, night after night, can affect many parts of a child's body and growth—and all aspects of her life.

Lack of Motivation to Play

Younger children love to play. It is a natural instinct to want to discover, uncover, imagine, and see how the world works. As they get older, this may look different from when they were younger. An older child might want to ride her bike to a friend's house. Or she may like to video chat with a friend, talk on the phone, read a book, create, draw, play board games, go to the store to try on new clothes, attend a concert, and more. Each child is unique and has special talents, interests, and abilities.

Just like waking up in the middle of the night, the lack of motivation to play at home or outside of the home is not a red flag by itself. Some children get bored. Others' interests and abilities change with time. However, if your child looks sad, zoned out, or lifeless, then you need to dig deeper. Everyone has sad days and hard days, but if there are more sad/bad days than happy days, something is going on. Your child could be experiencing depression from the hurt she is experiencing through bullying. This does not mean she will struggle with depression all her life. It means something is keeping her from being herself, and she needs someone to help her find her hope and light again.

Detaching from or Avoiding Enjoyable Activities

Have you noticed your child tuning out and looking like she is in "another world?" This is what is meant by detaching. When a child—or anyone else—does this, she is thinking about something. She is not verbalizing what is playing inside her head. As you saw in "The Attic," any emotion and any story could be playing on repeat in her mind's eye. It can be something that happened that day or something that happened months or years ago. Something left an imprint on her brain, and it hasn't gone away.

Children can have days in which they do not feel well. They also can be worn out from a strenuous day of exercise, such as after the first dance practice of the season or after a recital. Those days, however, are not what we are talking about here. We're referring to the times when fun is happening all around your child, and she is not participating, maybe even not present in the moment at all. Her eyes may be wandering. Her facial expression may be downcast. She lays around. And when she speaks, her words are negative or critical. Overall, she seems depressed or exhausted.

In addition to detaching from activities, your child may also avoid activities that she used to enjoy. For example, maybe your child has always loved to play basketball. Whenever she got the chance, she'd shoot hoops. When you suggest, day after day, she goes outside to play basketball, she has an excuse for why she can't play. Or she may go so far to say it's a "dumb sport."

"I don't like basketball anymore."

This can be a sign something must have happened when she last played basketball. For example, Jenny [again, false name] may have said, "Oh, look _____ [your child's name] can't make a shot. She's such a terrible basketball player," or a classmate might not have picked her to be on her team. The classmate possibly didn't choose her just to be mean, but your child internalized it and heard the message, "I'm terrible at basketball!" Now she believes that lie even though you know she is one of the best players on her basketball team and makes many of the team's baskets. And it was historically an activity that lit her up.

Avoiding Homework

Each child is different when it comes to homework. Some love doing math homework because they love math. Others love reading homework when they get to choose their book. As long as there is a routine in the home regarding when and how to complete homework, most children will do it even if it isn't their favorite subject. Some need a little coaxing, but most elementary-age students are compliant. However, some children refuse to do homework, and this behavior alone is not a sign they are being bullied.

What matters is a change. With the vast majority, suddenly avoiding homework is something to note, especially if they are showing any of the other behaviors. For example, our daughter knew that after she had a snack and had an hour to play, she was to complete her homework before dinner. When she was being bullied, she would fight us, not wanting to honor the routine. Through probing questions, we learned the homework did not include hard concepts for her. Instead, she was exhausted from the events of the school day (being bullied), and she had no more energy or brain power to complete her homework. Other times, she would go to her room to read and get away, then forget she had homework to complete. When this happened, she would wake up frantic and remain stressed throughout her morning routine. Or she would be emotional on her way to school because she did not finish her homework. That just added more stress to her body and set her up for not wanting to go to school at all.

Being Forgetful

Most children have an amazing ability to remember a lot of things. Their memory is a lot better than most adults. I am not sure if this is because they are still growing or if it is because they do not have as many responsibilities to remember. Most children are sponges, and they have a large brain capacity—able to learn and hold a lot of information. They are human, though, and they can forget things from time to time.

What we want to focus on here is when your child gets *very* forgetful. She suddenly forgets several things. These can be simple things like where she put an article of clothing, where her backpack is, or what she went to the kitchen to get. The more complex things she may forget are what she likes to do, tasks she is supposed to complete, food she likes to eat, and so on. Everyone forgets things from time to time. When your child forgets one thing after another, and it's adding up, it should make you wonder why. This is especially true for the more complex things. If your child cannot remember the more complex things, this could be a sign of an identity crisis or that something is causing her brain not to function properly.

Ignoring Daily Chores

As children grow older, they typically have daily chores or household tasks they are increasingly responsible for. They can be as simple as putting away toys they have played with and progress to more complex tasks, such as unloading and loading the dishwasher, washing counters, taking out the trash, or cleaning an entire bathroom or bedroom. When it is a daily or weekly occurrence, they know when and how it is supposed to be done.

Children do not always like doing chores. No one does. However, most children do not want the natural consequences that come with not completing them. When a child is being bullied, she does not care about the natural consequences of not completing the task, or even more obvious, she may not have the capacity to remember there is a consequence for not finishing the task. Instead, her mind is burned out from the day.

Some children have favorite chores. For example, my daughter loves to do dishes, and I have a son who loves to take out the trash. These are things they enjoy tackling and that help them release stress. (I don't know why, but we aren't complaining, right!?) When your child is not completing the daily chores or household tasks she enjoys, this should be a warning sign, signaling, "Hey, something is up. She usually loves to _____."

Not Completing Simple Tasks

If you detect this behavior, I consider this a *giant red flag*! When your child cannot complete simple tasks that she has been doing for some time, something is definitely wrong. For example, if she cannot brush her teeth, choose clothes to wear, tie her shoes, remember where to put something in her room, or remember how to do a simple activity she normally does involuntarily as a habit, something is amiss.

She is likely depressed. Her brain is running in survival mode, and she is having a hard time doing and thinking through simple tasks. This could be coupled with crying and forgetfulness. For example, if she cannot find her toothpaste (even though it's in its normal spot), she has tears rolling down her face. She is not really sad that she can't find her toothpaste; she is overwhelmed or worried about the day ahead. She can't even grab the toothpaste out of the cabinet because thoughts of the bullying are storming through her brain like a tornado uprooting a tree.

When a child exhibits this behavior, it is in the family's best interest to seek a counselor or professional adult outside the home and normal influence—someone who will remain unbiased to her and her current circumstance. A person who is gifted and trained in uncovering, releasing, and working through trauma, emotionally, mentally, and potentially physically. Many individuals have been trained in this area, and there should be an expert within driving distance who can help your child.

We are getting ready to leave the Living Room. I remember feeling the flood of emotions as I unpacked all of my daughter's feelings. I remember feeling helpless. Feeling somewhat hopeless. Feeling very desperate. Shame overtook me, and I felt like her struggle was my fault. I should have known better. I should have seen all the signs. Many times, I said to myself—and then to my husband—"I am her mom. I should have seen all this unfolding. I should know better. Is my daughter broken beyond repair?" Even as I type this, tears well up in my eyes, thinking about the day I realized our daughter was being bullied, and the bullies had caused my child to forget her true identity. It felt like such a debilitating punch to the gut, and it was hard to take a deep breath and think about what to do next without panicking.

So . . . I give you permission to walk through what you need to, emotion-wise, as her mama or parent. Feel all the feels you need to feel right now. No parent wants her child to hurt like this. No parent wants her child to lose her special spark. Grieve what has happened for just a moment if you need to. Bullying affects the whole family, not just the one who is bullied.

When you are ready, take a deep breath in and a gentle breath out. Dry your tears and blow your nose. Release it all. I am proud of you. You just dug down deep and got messy with your child. Well done, Mama! You took a big, bold step for your child. You reminded her to stand in Truth. To live out her true identity. You reminded her that you are and will always be an advocate for her.

The difficult work is not yet done, though. This is the beginning of your healing journey—one you'll take together. Open the door. Walk out and into your office. You are now going to work to find a counselor who will help you and your child release, heal, and repair. Please remember, I am here with you, Mama. You are not alone in this next step.

Home Office Door

You now know something is going on, but perhaps you've realized you cannot help your child through your own strength or means. Take a moment to accept this. It is okay. When we have a broken arm, we don't sit at home, trying to snap the bone back into place. Instead, we go to the doctor, have him evaluate our arm, and follow his directions. The same is true when our child is sick with a high fever. As good parents, we don't sit at home, allow our children to writhe in pain or discomfort, self-diagnose for weeks, and let our children get severely sick—or worse, die.

When a child is being bullied, this strategy of finding professional help holds. Your child needs to navigate the pain, hidden emotions, the lies that have been stored in her brain, and everything that goes with that with someone who has been trained to guide her. You love your child dearly; that is why you are still reading. Maybe it's time to go further. You will do your child and yourself a favor by seeking a professional with tools you have not used before. And if you are brutally honest, you need that help too. Bullying doesn't just affect the one being bullied. It also affects those who live with the survivor.

Factors to Consider When Choosing a Counselor

There are many factors to consider when choosing a counselor. Some factors may be easier to decide on, while others will take a little more thought. These factors fall into three categories: your child, their school, and the counselor.

For the child, you need to consider gender, age, specific needs, and the type of counseling you prefer . . . also, where you live, your insurance coverage, and financial resources. For the school, you need to take note of how much support is already provided and if the administrators are willing to provide more. When looking at the counselor, you must consider the gender of the counselor, their educational background, any academic accolades or professional specialties, and maybe even the personal or spiritual beliefs from which the counselor teaches or works.

Let's first consider the child's gender. Boys and girls learn differently. Their brains are wired differently, and they accept help and feedback in varying ways. However, no two girls or boys are the same. These are the *generalizations* for both genders: Girls tend to be more emotional or "hormonal," feel the need to talk through and unpack their emotions, take criticism more personally, and have a lot they are thinking about inside their brains. Boys have feelings too. However, it isn't as common for them to experience their emotions—have outward expressions of those feelings—as it is for girls. Most boys do not take feedback as critically as girls, and their brains compartmentalize things. They typically think of one thing at a time instead of multiple ideas or events simultaneously. They have a "tunnel vision" that helps them stay deeply engaged on one task or event, unlike most girls.

When you are considering your child's gender and how it might affect counseling success, you must decide if the gender of the counselor also matters. For example, I don't believe my daughter would have experienced as many breakthroughs with a male counselor. She trusts women more with her feelings; she relates better to women when sharing "the deep things," and she feels more comfortable around women in a professional or medical setting. One of my sons learns best from his dad, but he opens up more to women he trusts, such as me or his grandma. His dad loves him, but my son believes he needs to be strong around his dad and will look weak if he shares his feelings or can't problem-solve through the deep stuff himself. This is not because of my husband's personality but just an innate disposition my son harbors to be a strong male among other males. You know your child best and how she is wired. It all comes down to who your child trusts most and if the gender of your child and the gender of the counselor make a difference in the amount of healing and breakthrough your child will gain.

Let's talk about age. A child's brain grows differently at each stage of life. In addition, the child's short- and long-term memory are formed differently at each stage. During the start of the elementary years through age seven, children learn best through play, tactile learning, hands-on learning, and role-playing. At about age seven, they can repeat learned information because their memory bank becomes stronger. Additionally, they learn social-emotional skills and problem-solving skills through their play.

As a child matures and enters the preteen stage, she learns best through communication, hearing, and doing since she can now reason logically. In the adolescent years, starting at about eleven and going through the teen years, children can reason hypothetically. Therefore, they can think logically through possible scenarios and consider problems and solutions for those scenarios. Because of these developmental markers, you have to take into account the age of your child and how her brain is developing to determine the best type of therapy for your child.

The third factor is the type of counseling you would like your child to receive. There are multiple parts to this factor. One is personality. How does she learn best? For a young child, *play therapy* tends to be a better avenue. Her brain cannot think abstractly, so physically playing with toys, such as puppets, stuffed animals, or dolls, will help her work through her emotions and what she has experienced. A good counselor will not sit with a four-year-old and say, "Tell me what happened. What did John do to you?" and expect the child to talk through everything. The counselor may ask the child questions, but he knows a young child learns best through play and concrete ideas. Therefore, play therapy—when the therapist gets on the floor or down to the child's level to play with her—is the best form of counseling for a young child. Then, through play, the child naturally expresses and works through their emotions, talking through them and their corresponding situations—and hopefully learns to practice coping strategies through play.

Another form of counseling that helps younger children is *art therapy*. In art therapy, a professional art therapist helps children find alternative ways to express themselves. It gives voice to children's experiences through painting, drawing, clay design, or whatever mode of creation is used to model what each child has been through and is feeling. This form of therapy empowers the child by helping her release what she has been experiencing and holding inside and sharing it with a trained counselor and parent.

In addition to the child's age, the type of counseling offered can depend on the trauma the child experienced. As discussed in "School Entrance Doors," there are different forms of bullying. If a child has received psychological bullying, the words spoken over her can be stored in her memory and must be slowly brought into the light to be addressed appropriately. The best type of counseling for that is *trauma-informed counseling*. Trauma-informed counseling is a specific type of therapy that recognizes how the traumatic experience impacts the child's whole well-being: the mental, behavioral, emotional, physical, and spiritual dimensions. This type of therapy is rooted in the connection between the traumatic experience and the emotional and behavioral responses of the child. The main purpose of this type of counseling is to offer skills and strategies that help a child understand, process, cope with, and create a healthy meaning for the traumatic experiences and the emotions and memories felt during that time. Then they can develop healthier ways to survive what they have experienced, moving forward in freedom. Trauma-informed counseling is also beneficial for a child who has been physically bullied.

If a child no longer trusts an adult because of a professional or caregiver not keeping them safe or advocating for them, another form of therapy that should be considered is *attachment therapy*. This type of therapy helps a child rebuild trust in adult relationships and focuses on expressing emotions. Sometimes it is a form of therapy that can be used within trauma-informed counseling. One strategy of attachment therapy will be shared in the "Counselor's Office Door."

The next factor is how much support your school provides. If your child goes to a school that has a school counselor, your child might not need as much outside professional counseling. The professional counselor and school counselor can work together. That is assuming that the school counselor has the appropriate education and experience and is willing to advocate for your child, allot valuable time for the healing process for your child, and is well-trained in helping a child who has been bullied.

When considering school counselors, you need to ask yourself and the school some targeted questions. How well do I trust the school counselor? Is he or she approachable? Are they willing to take time to meet with me or are they always talking about how busy they are? Do they naturally appreciate and respect my child? What is their background and what degree(s) do they have? Do they have a child of their own? (A counselor does not have to have children to be a good fit, but I can share from experience this adds another layer of understanding if they are parents themselves.) Is the counseling office welcoming and private? How often is the counselor in the classroom? Are they willing to be a team player?

I outline two scenarios that explain why I think you should ask these questions. As a former elementary school teacher and a mom of four children, I have experienced two types of counselors.

Some counselors have been amazing advocates for my child or their students. I have also worked with others who are more invested in their paychecks than in the well-being of the children who need their support. Just because a school counselor has a degree to teach in your child's school, it does not mean that he or she will be an advocate for your child—unfortunately. I learned that the hard way as a teacher and as a parent!

When I was a child, we had an amazing elementary school counselor. When he walked into our classroom, we were excited to see him because he brought a smile and warmth to the room, and that made us feel comfortable. He taught us in fun, interactive ways that excited us and made us look forward to the days he came in. He educated us on a variety of topics, including peer pressure, confidence, bullying, sexual abuse, saying no to drugs, feelings, and so much more. He formed such a community of trust through his listening ears and his caring heart that at least I felt comfortable coming to him with the joys in my life and the difficult situations. In addition, he had an incentive where we could earn lunch with him and a group of friends. In essence, we got small group time with him, and we came away feeling seen, heard, and valued. His door was always open to us, and, at least as children, we never felt like he was too busy to help us even if it was a last-minute situation.

On the flip side, at one of the schools where I taught, there was a school counselor who did not advocate for her students. As a teacher, I did not trust her to share life events, let alone entrust my students who needed someone who would truly listen and help them to her. She seemed annoyed about having to come to school and work with students. When a student needed to meet with her, she was unapproachable. She rarely smiled and rushed them in and out of her office in the least amount of time possible. This counselor's background was in middle school "something or another," and she did not have additional training to handle bullying. Her education and personality did not work well with younger children. She tried hard to avoid the classrooms because she didn't "like the students' ages," and it made more work for her in the form of research and lesson plans for the weeks ahead. So she was not trustworthy, approachable, respectful, available, or an advocate for most of the students in the school.

Where you live is the next factor to consider when choosing a counselor. Think of where you live, work, and attend school in correlation to where the counselor practices. How far are you willing to drive? How much school will your child miss? What hours are they open? How many counselors are available in your area? What types of counselors are available in your area? How many clients do they take on? Are there counselors who practice independently or in a bigger practice? Who is the owner? If you live in a small town, typically people know each other's business more than if you live in a big city (speaking from experience). There may be a good counselor locally, but if you do not trust the owner, that counselor may not be a good fit because you want your child's sessions and information to be kept confidential. If you live in a small town, there may not be best-fit professional counselors, so you will need to look in the next bigger city.

I challenge you to be vulnerable and reach out to local people you trust as you are considering where you live. Online reviews are helpful if you have no one to ask. However, friends and family you know well and trust can sometimes recommend a good professional counselor. Your child's school (if it is a trustworthy one), a local church, a nonprofit organization, or other helpful people or organizations may have recommendations for good counselors. For my daughter, I reached out to a friend who had a child my daughter's age, and I asked her if she knew of any good counselors that she thought would be a good fit for my daughter and our family.

Another factor to consider is the insurance you carry (or not) and your financial resources. Every insurance plan has in-network and out-of-network options. Those who are in-network are covered partially or fully by your insurance policy. Whereas, the out-of-network counselors will not be covered by your insurance. You can ask your insurance company who is in your network. This will provide you with a list, and then you can go back and consider the above factors when choosing from that list. If you are going with an out-of-network counselor, you must decide how much money you can invest in your child. Your child's healing journey is crucial—and worth a lot—but you don't want to go bankrupt or find yourself unable to pay for your family's other needs.

The final piece to consider when choosing a counselor is the educational background; academic accolades and specialties; and professional, personal, and possibly spiritual beliefs the counselor offers and centers his teaching around. What a counselor knows, believes, and does will affect the results your child experiences in the counseling sessions. On the counselor's website, there should be a short biography or a section that explains his or her educational background and academic accolades. When I was choosing a counselor for my child, these were a big factor I took into account before choosing who I thought would be the best fit for my child. Some counselors I had been referred to seemed great, but they were not trained in trauma counseling, bullying, or other things I felt were important. Or they did not have any professional experience working with the age range my daughter fell into. In addition to background and accolades, there are beliefs to consider. These can be spiritual beliefs, school beliefs, and counseling best-practice beliefs. For our family, it was important to choose a counselor who shared the same spiritual beliefs as us because then she could use Scripture to renew our daughter's mind during the healing journey. In addition, we did not want our daughter to practice other activities against her spiritual upbringing.

Choosing a Counselor

Now that you have considered all the factors and weighed many options, it is time to act on the information. First, make a list of all the counselors that meet your criteria. Rank them from the best choice on down. Then gather all of their information and contact numbers. After that, make a list of important questions to ask them. For example, "Are you taking new clients?" Where are they located? How long are the sessions? How do they help children who are bullied? What type of therapy do they provide? How often are the sessions? Do they accept your insurance? How soon can your child start? Do parents sit in on the sessions? How do they support the family or parents? Is your child assigned to one counselor or a team of professionals? Are there interns that will work with your child?

Once you have written down your questions, you need to figure out the best way to contact the counselor. Some counselors prefer you first reach out via email, through their website, while others would like to have a connection call to see if you and they are a good fit. I think a phone call is the best avenue. You can hear the tone of the counselor's voice, ask as many questions as you need to, and understand how they might communicate with you. A lot can be learned from a simple phone call. For example, I had a phone call with one counselor who came highly recommended. In the short conversation we had, she did not seem welcoming, and I felt like she was in a hurry to end the conversation. This counselor did not seem to be a good fit for me or my daughter, as she did not even value the time we had together in that short call.

After you have connected with all the counselors on your list, you must decide who is the best fit for your child and family. To choose wisely, list the pros and cons of each one. For example, when looking at "Sally's" information, a pro is that she has a background in working with children who have gone through trauma, but a con is that she can only meet with your child once a month.

Next, rank them from top to bottom, with the top being the ones who have the most pros. After that, make an appointment with the top counselor. Overall, when you choose a counselor, they should provide you with the most hope for moving forward.

> *Take a moment to take a deep breath in and a gentle breath out. You took a big leap toward the healing process for your child—and honestly, for you too. This is the step most parents do not take. They don't want to let others in. They do not want to admit they need help. They believe the lie that says they have to figure this out and solve this alone because they are the parents. Or they do not want to take time out of their day to drive their child to sessions and possibly share their struggles with another person. I am very proud of you for loving your child so much that you would reach out, ask for, and accept help. I have tears in my eyes remembering how hard this was for me, to lay down my pride and pick up hope for my child. I am so very proud of you and would love to give you a giant hug, high-five, fist bump, handshake, or whatever else would show you the gratitude I have for you as a parent who puts their child's needs above their own pride. Well done!*

Counselor's Office Door

You and your child are now ready to take your first outside step in your healing journey together. Many emotions may be flooding your body. You may feel totally out of control, and that may scare you (it sure did me). You may feel defeated because you are the mama or parent who used to be able to kiss boo-boos away or hug your little one and make her know all is well in her little world again. You used to be able to bring that smile back with the simplest of actions: a hug, a kiss, a tickle, a joke, or a word that reminded her of her worth. And now . . . you feel helpless.

However, you are here because you have at least a small measure of hope that the counselor you have chosen has the educational background and the right tools to meet your daughter where she is and help her move forward.

Every child needs two basic things. The first basic need is a sense of *belonging*. Belonging is "feeling emotionally connected and part of a group."[9] The second basic need is *significance*, which is "feeling sufficiently great or important to be worthy of attention; noteworthy."[10] Your sweet one has been robbed of both, and now is the time to get that back! It may not happen in a day, but please stay along for the ride for however long it takes. *Every child* should and needs to feel a sense of belonging and significance, and your child is no different.

As you sit in the counselor's office lobby, use your senses to take note of what is around you. Plant your feet and feel grounded. Take a deep breath in and a deep breath out. Let out all of the emotions you've bottled up at home so you don't "lose it." What do you see around you? Usually, the counselor's office has inspirational art, quotes, books, and colors that bring peace and tranquility. What do you smell? In our counselor's office lobby, there were calming and beautiful-smelling essential oils, gently sprayed into the air from a diffuser. What do you hear? Ours had light piano music, inspirational songs, and noise machines, sending out gentle sounds of ocean waves. Sometimes there was stillness, with everyone sitting without talking (those were the best days—the opportunities to sit in peace and breathe). What do you feel? The hug of a pillow, the softness of a couch, or the cushion of a chair you sink into?

This should be a place you look forward to visiting every week. It is going to be the area where you and your child get to let it all out and lay it all down. Yes, there will be a wave of emotions you never thought you could feel in one setting or in one hour. But this is the place you get to heal—*together*! As long as you and your child are willing to open up, this is where your child will reclaim her identity and pick her true self back up. The unique, wonderful, smart, beautiful, chosen, _____ [insert your child's name] who is created for so much more!

Intake Assessment

As the counselor calls your child's name, any emotion you feel is normal. Sadness? Yes, I felt that one. Anger? Yep, been there. Shame? Felt that one also—until our counselor reminded me that shame was never meant for us to feel or hold. Hope? Yes, I felt like I was holding on to the last thread of hope at that moment. No child and no parent is meant to walk in all this pain and grief, but hold on. There is abundant *hope* on the other side.

A good counselor will not dive straight into a tool or engage in a deep counseling session on the first day. Instead, the counselor or team should do an intake first. This helps the counselor get a snapshot of what has happened, how your child feels, measure the likelihood of depression, know if your child is at risk for suicide, understand how you feel, learn what brought your child and you to this day, and observe your child. This is not a judgmental time at all. Instead, think of it like visiting any other doctor's office. When you take your child in, the doctor wants to get the whole picture before determining the best treatment options. The doctor moves through the typical steps like taking a temperature, measuring height, weighing your child, and looking in her eyes and ears. A great counselor has a similar assessment routine to come up with the clearest plan of action and the right tools to help you and your child best.

While the counselor does the intake assessment, you have two roles. First, listen in, but do not share anything unless you are asked. You may get a glimpse inside your child's head and learn some thoughts you haven't heard yet (this happened to me). Second, be an added voice and advocate when called upon. Your child may not be ready to share certain things, answer some of the questions that bring back traumatic responses, or share some of the information that has been difficult because your child has become numb to it, possibly forgotten it. However, let the counselor and child lead the discussion. For example, if the counselor asks, "Have you ever done anything mean to a peer?" Do not interject, "Oh, no, my daughter is the nicest child and would never do such a thing."

After the intake is over, be okay with no answers at this point. Instead, the counselor or counseling team will set up a time for you to meet and have your first official counseling session. In addition, they may tell you how often the counselor wants to meet—for example, weekly. The counselor will let you know they need a certain amount of days to evaluate the intake, come up with the next steps, and formulate a game plan for moving forward. They may give you some ideas or things to watch out for until your next session, especially if your child has suicidal thoughts.

First Session

Several thoughts may rush through your mind as you wait for your first official counseling session. What does the counselor see in my child? How are they going to fix this? Do they think I am a bad parent? Can they really help us or is this all just a waste of time? Instead of staying in your head, ask your child how she feels. Is she nervous about anything? Does she want you to sit with her in her session? Remind her that she can trust the counselor. The counselor will not share anything talked about each day with anyone other than her and you. Try to reassure your child that she is safe, loved, seen, heard, and valued.

She likely has many thoughts and emotions she doesn't know what to do with and feels like she is on trial right now. Getting ready to sit in the judgment seat. She is not in a judgment seat at all, but the child who was bullying has made her believe she is. More than likely, deep down she believes the lie that this is her fault, which is far from the truth.

The noise in your head stops as the counselor calls your child's name. You both stand up and take deep breaths as you walk to the counselor's room. You never thought you would be here, and neither did she. If the counselor has asked to speak to your child alone, then you can request to sit in. Your child may have lost all trust in adults, and she might need to build that trust again. That is completely normal and part of the process.

As you walk into the room, it begins. Every counselor does things differently, so I cannot share exactly what your session is going to look like or feel like. However, I can give you a glimpse of what my daughter's amazing counselor was like and what we worked through. If you are not getting the same care and support we did (or that you expect), I challenge you to look elsewhere for a counselor. Remember, we wanted a counselor who shared our same spiritual beliefs, as I felt this was also a spiritual battle. You may not feel the same way, but this was important to me for my daughter's healing journey.

Our counselor started by making my daughter feel seen, valued, and heard. She asked open-ended questions to get to know my daughter personally. What were her favorite things to do or play with at home? Favorite things at school? What color did she like? (She asked this one for selecting materials and even dry-erase marker colors for illustrations as she taught my daughter coping skills.) She brought out a bucketful of fidget toys and even noted which ones my daughter gravitated toward.

After getting our daughter to open up through surface-level questions, our counselor wanted our daughter to know her worth. She wanted her to know that what was done to her was not her fault. That it was a choice made by the child who was bullying, and that child who was bullying was choosing to belittle her. The child who was bullying was mean and purposely wanted to hurt our daughter. Instead of stopping there, the counselor shared scriptures and "I am" statements with our daughter so she could start replacing the negative thoughts in her head with truths straight from the Word of God. A few of these were "I am worthy. I am loved. I am unique." More of these "I am" statements paired with Scripture will be shared in more detail in the chapter "Child's Bathroom Door," along with a free printable resource.

Once these truths were explained and reinforced, the counselor had our daughter choose her two favorites or the two she wanted to think about and say to herself until her next counseling session. The counselor wrote down the two on her whiteboard and then had our daughter repeat them several times. They talked about how when the child who was bullying said the opposite, our daughter could think about those truths instead. Then, as she got brave enough, she could say them out loud to the child who was bullying to counter the negative verbal assault. This was just one way to rewire her brain.

In addition to the "I am" statements, the counselor had us start something this first session that would carry over into every other session moving forward. She had our daughter use what the counselor called "buzzies." This was a tool our daughter held in her hands or put in her shoes. As she had our daughter say the truth or a strategy she was taught, these buzzies would produce a gentle vibration in our daughter's hands or feet. It was not an electric shock but a sensation that research has shown helps people rewire their brains and create new nerve patterns to better keep new information in their short- and long-term memories. It was similar to the feeling of sitting in a massage chair or putting your hand on a drying machine. The buzzies are part of a specific therapy modality called Eye Movement Desensitization and Reprocessing (EMDR) that uses slow, bilateral stimulation to strengthen the positive things a parent says to the child. This can be an important part of attachment therapy and one option a parent can consider when seeking a therapist for their child.

After repeating the truths or practicing the tools or strategies, the counselor ended the sessions by having me, the parent, speak truth over our daughter. Usually, I was supposed to think about the previous week and choose at least two things that I was proud of her for. To be completely transparent here: the first few weeks and some other days further into our counseling sessions, this task was difficult because our daughter had been working through some extreme emotions at home, especially anger, and living with her—and her emotions—was draining. The things I chose were not supposed to be chores that she was asked to do in the house; instead, they were supposed to be character builders and actions that we wanted to see more of at home. Two examples were, "This week you came up with a fun imaginative game to play with your brother, and you made him smile and laugh. That made him feel so happy, and he loved spending time with his big sister," and "I am very proud of how you reacted when your brother messed with your toys, and it made you mad. Instead of yelling at him and shoving him, you walked back to your room and read a book to calm down."

The Internal Tornado

Once the counselor built rapport and our daughter began to trust her, she shared a new concept my daughter and I had not heard about before. The internal tornado, which I've touched on earlier. When children and adults alike stuff their emotions, those emotions brew and brew inside like a tornado that builds in intensity over time. As the internal tornado grows, it reaches the point where it has to come out, and that is the explosive or "big emotions" that erupt on the outside for all to see. The emotions that come out from the internal tornado are not necessarily what started the tornado. For example, if a girl is being psychologically bullied, she likely feels sad because of the meanness—from being excluded from groups and the unkind notes filled with lies about her passed around school. At the moment, she feels emotionally hurt, but by the time she gets home, that sadness and rejection have brewed into something fierce. When her brother leaves his shoe right by the door and she trips and falls, instead of blowing it off as something minor, she yells at her brother and shoves him for leaving his shoes at the door. What could have been a slight frustration has turned into loud yelling and her hurting her brother.

When the child cannot share these emotions at school, she empties them at home, usually as big outbursts. As a parent, this can feel overwhelming—as though you can't do anything right. That your child is always angry, yelling, or extremely sad. You want your home to be a safe place for your child to come home to, but you don't want it to take on a negative atmosphere. If left unchecked, your home can become a toxic environment if the "tornados" do not simmer down or stop forming altogether.

What can the child do to avoid letting these tornadoes form and spin out of control? The most effective way is to become aware of how her body feels when she is experiencing these emotions. For example, when she is feeling angry, she scowls, her cheeks and her chest get tight, her shoulders stiffen, her fists clench, her heart races, and her breaths become short. As she notices these reactions in her body, she can call it what it is. "I am feeling *angry*." Not, "I am an angry person," but "I am *feeling* angry."

> **Becoming aware of how her body feels when experiencing strong emotions will help avoid tornadic outbursts.**

After she acknowledges how her body holds this emotion internally and names the feeling for what it is, the child practices—when she is calm—the proper steps for defusing the big feeling so it doesn't erupt. For example, she can say, "I am angry because _____." She names the emotion and what has caused it. Now, instead of going into fight, flight, freeze, or flee mode like she usually does when she is angry, she can say, "I am safe" and counter the feelings with the opposite of what made her angry. So, if the child who is bullying her calls her "dumb" at school and makes her mad, then she can practice by saying, "I am safe," which sends her brain the message that she doesn't need to fight, flight, freeze, or flee. Then she will say, "I am a smart girl because _____[insert something she knows she is smart in or something she does that is smart]." This reframing takes her body out of high-alert mode and rewires her brain to focus on the truth.

Some other strategies she could use are breathing techniques, such as breathing in for five seconds, holding for three seconds, and breathing out for ten seconds, or taking a breath in for ten seconds, then breathing out like a lion until it's gone. The exhaled breath calms the nervous system down, so the exhaled breath should be longer than the inhale breath. A third option is belly breathing. One way is taking deep breaths in, filling her belly to the count of ten, holding for two seconds, and breathing out for ten seconds. She can repeat this nine more times. This gets her to focus on taking deep breaths and counting instead of relenting to her feelings and erupting.

The important piece in this is that the child practices often outside of experiencing the emotion. That way, when a big emotion like anger comes, she has already stored in her short-term memory a healthy coping strategy for calming down.

Many kids and families have a code word, something the child or a parent can say at home that reminds the child, "I am angry and I need to _____ [whatever she has practiced before the emotion erupts]. This should be agreed upon by her and not something you do for her without permission. If she hasn't agreed, you saying the word could be another trigger, adding fuel to the fire instead of helping her calm down.

Finding Her Uniqueness Again

Everyone has emotions every day, but the first step in helping a child navigate those emotions is teaching her to discern how the emotion feels inside her body, understanding the reaction(s) it causes, and practicing how to keep the emotion from reaching the "red zone," where she erupts with a big reaction. Once that

> **Help her notice how the emotions feel inside her body to keep herself out of the "red zone."**

is practiced over time, a counselor can build the child's sense of identity. Sometimes the child who is bullying has torn down the child and made her feel so small that she forgets what makes her unique and why that uniqueness is special. Finding herself again may take some time.

One exercise that works wonders to help a child find her uniqueness is writing a timeline of her life. The counselor draws a horizontal line on a big sheet of paper. Then she helps the child plot major events, positive or negative, on the paper. The first event should be her birth. The counselor smiles and happily announces, "On _____ day in _____ year, _____ was born, and her parents were very excited that a sweet baby girl was born." This connects the child back to her parents with a strong positive emotion (which may be needed as these big emotions and reactions at home have exhausted everyone). With the next events the child remembers, they discuss at length what emotion comes with those events. For example, the child might share that she started dance class or had her first dance recital. She felt happy to start or proud that she completed the routine. She loved that everyone cheered; her parents gave her big hugs, and others praised her. This brings back positive feelings for her and reminds her that she is a good dancer. Not everyone is a good dancer, so this is something that sets her apart from others. It makes her uniquely her.

By doing this exercise, it opens the child's eyes to when she no longer felt unique. It shows her what specific event occurred and who disrupted her positive self-worth. It may bring about sadness, grief, and other big emotions. However, unlike at school, the child is now in a safe place to release and work through those emotions, allowing her to practice handling them in a healthy manner. She gets to notice and discuss how that event feels in her body and learn what to do to feel better again.

A second way for a child to find her uniqueness is a game called "Totem." The child and the parent each get five cards. They read the cards and choose the best two that describe the other person. For example, the parent gets the cards "funny," "thoughtful," "authentic," "playful," and "perceptive." Mom narrows it down to the two cards she thinks most closely describe her child. Then she reads those two cards out loud and chooses the one that best characterizes her child. The parent and child take turns sharing the most appropriate card they've chosen for the other person and explain why. In the end, both the child and the parent get to tell each other about positive personality traits they like in each other. It is a win-win for both because the child needs positive affirmation spoken over her—and so does the parent because both have worked through trauma during the bullying journey. Additionally, this gives you, the parent, more ideas of how to praise and verbally tell your child how proud you are of her at home.

Equipping the Child

Once the child has recognized the brewing tornado and emotions, practiced calming strategies, heard truth spoken over her life, and learned how her uniqueness is a positive thing, she is ready to become equipped to counter any future attacks by the child who is bullying. This may look different for each individual, depending on which form of bullying is happening to her. Some of the tactics will be the same for all forms of bullying, while others will be specific to the type taking place.

The first tactic is to identify *where* the bullying is taking place. If it is happening in a place where there is not enough adult supervision, she needs to do one of two things: avoid these areas in the school when an adult is not present or keep herself out of those situations altogether. If she cannot avoid it altogether, then she needs to be sure she always has a friend or group of friends with her who will be her allies. It mustn't be another student who is being bullied by the same child who is bullying. If it is, then both will become targets. Tactic number two is thinking about what emotion arises when the child who is bullying targets her. This one is to be used for all forms of bullying *except* physical bullying. When someone is getting physically bullied, she needs to get away and report it immediately to an adult so immediate action can be taken.

Usually, the emotion triggered is anger, fear, or sadness. These emotions reward the child who is bullying for his actions and keep him coming back for more. That may sound sick, but it is the truth. The child who is bullying wants the victim to feel one of these strong emotions so he feels like he has power over his peer. Once the emotion is acknowledged, the survivor (not *victim*) needs to learn how to exercise a great deal of restraint to avoid showing that emotion. Once "the bully has figured out that a particular target is no longer easy to knock down, he'll give up."[11] I am not saying teach your child to no longer feel emotion. Instead, I am sharing the strategy of how to show a counter-emotion that will disrupt the normal trend and confuse the child who is bullying into thinking he no longer has the upper hand. Harber, whom I quoted above, additionally shares in his book, *Bullyproof Your Child for Life*, these proven ways to counter-react to a child who is bullying:

1. Smile.
2. Laugh off criticism.
3. Make a new friend.
4. Stand up for self without whining, yelling, crying, or trying to insult the bully.
5. Show no emotional or behavioral reaction to bullying.[12]

Tactic three is for physical bullying. If the child who is bullying tries to physically harm a child, the child being bullied needs permission to stand up for herself and get away. This may sound like a no-brainer. However, you would be surprised by how many students I have taught—and my own child—who heard all their lives to *be kind* and mistakenly think self-defense is unkind. I will give you an example from our daughter's life. The main child who was bullying her during her fourth-grade year shoved her. She did not do anything to defend herself. Then, later that day, she shared with me what happened. I explained to her that she was right in that I did not want her to purposely cause harm to the student who was bullying her. However, I wanted her to stand up for herself so harm didn't come to her, such as hitting her head on the ground. Later that same year, the child who was bullying my daughter blocked her from running up the playset stairs while she was engaged in a game of tag with her peers. The girl went to shove my daughter off the three-foot-tall slide set, and my daughter could have been severely hurt. However, she remembered what we had talked about, and she pushed the girl to get her off of her own, then jumped as the girl tried to shove her and went on playing with her other friends.

The fourth tactic goes with all forms of bullying. Find another friend or group of peers to play with. I am not saying let the child who is bullying control who plays with whom and that your child needs to make new friends while the child bullying gets to do whatever he wants. I am saying, even for a short time, your child may need to keep herself out of particular situations and group settings until the child who is bullying backs off. For example, the child can find another group of girls to jump rope with. She still gets to jump rope like she wants to at recess, but she is doing it away from the child who is targeting her during recess. Also, making new friends takes power away from the child who is bullying because your child is no longer alienated and looked down upon. Who knows, by her choosing to walk away from a certain group of friends, the others inside that group who are too scared to stand up for themselves may see an outlet for themselves and join her in the new group. My daughter experienced this firsthand during this challenging year.

The fifth tactic is to have a code word with a teacher or staff member who is around your child where the bullying tends to happen. This helps your child not have to tell the story in front of the child who is bullying and not be called a tattletale or snitch. Additionally, the teacher becomes aware, keeps your child safe, watches the child who is bullying more closely or removes the child who is bullying from the situation altogether. This code word needs to be something that doesn't make sense to the child who is bullying. For example, you don't want the word to be *bully* or *mean*. Instead, it could be *chicken*—something that only makes sense to the authority figure and the child. In the "Classroom Door" and "Administrator's Door," I will share more strategies for teachers and staff, which they can implement to bring safety and dissolve bullying.

> *We are getting ready to leave the Counselor's Office Door. Before we leave this room, I want to share something our daughter's counselor shared with me early on, when my daughter was not present in the room, that has been imprinted on my brain. "Kids are not resilient! Instead, just like adults, kids are human; kids have a breaking point, and the enemy is real and is on the prowl to steal, kill, and destroy! Children sin, just like adults, and we, as adults, need to disciple them, listen to them, help them understand feelings are okay and that God made their bodies to feel, teach them how to navigate their feelings in a healthy manner, and work through the hard stuff!"[13]*
>
> *Remember that. No child is completely resilient.*
>
> *Now take a deep breath in and slowly let that breath out. I am so proud of you for loving and caring for your child so much that you did the hard work necessary to help rewire her brain—and yours. This is not a one-stop shop, though. You and she will likely need to revisit this room for months or years to come. And let me be the first to tell you, that is more than fine! That is healthy. My daughter's counselor has become a cherished soul in our family, and if it wasn't for her, I don't think my daughter would have come out on the other side. I definitely know I would not be here writing, especially with a smile on my face, as I think of this wonderful human being who breathed life back into my daughter, my heart and mind, and our home.*

7

Classroom Door

I want to give a disclaimer. There is no one-size-fits-all recommendation for when you should walk through this door. In our journey, we thought the teacher was going to be a strong advocate for our daughter, so we stepped through this door before walking through the "Counselor's Office Door." Our daughter's teacher was not well-trained in proper proactive and reactive steps to take when one of her students was experiencing bullying, and she was so overwhelmed with a personal family crisis that she was not operating out of her best teaching practices.

In addition, this classroom door may need to be stepped through several times in your journey to healing. You need to be a strong advocate for your child! Your child's voice is not being heard, so armor up as *you* now need to roar your mama's voice to push through all the noise and distractions preventing the teacher from keeping your child safe. As you prepare to walk through the "Classroom Door," school counselor and author Signe Whitson states in her book, *8 Keys to End Bullying*, "I'm not exaggerating when I tell parents to don their hero's cape and get ready to be *su-*

> "Parents, don your hero's cape and get ready to be superhuman, because in many cases, that is what challenging the status quo will take."
> —Signe Whitson

perhuman, because in many cases, that is what challenging the status quo will take. In every case, that is what their child deserves."[14]

As a former teacher, I can share with you that I did everything I could to keep my students safe and prevent bullying. However, even when a classroom teacher is fully rested and on alert, she cannot see and hear everything in every part of her classroom, on the playground, and during transitions throughout the day. That is why, as a former teacher, I plead with you as a parent to be the best advocate for your child. A good teacher understands you know your child best and will see how you want to be a team player. Educating a child takes the entire team: teacher, parent(s), support staff, counselor, and administration! *You* are a strong component of your child being seen, heard, and understood in the school. A great teacher wants to know if she is missing something and will want to be alerted if she is so she can provide the safest learning environment for your child. If you get a different reaction from any teacher, we will cover the proper steps to take in "Administrator's Door."

"By the time a young child has mustered the courage to tell an adult about the torment she has suffered at the hands of a peer, she has usually already exhausted all her coping skills. . . . When kids do talk about being bullied, it is imperative that parents honor the courageous act of sharing and become their child's *champion*."[15]

Whitson continues, "When a parent shows that she believes what her child has reported, takes the concerns seriously, and is willing to persistently stand up for her child, the child's self-worth can begin to grow again."[16]

> "When kids do talk about being bullied, it is imperative that parents honor the courageous act of sharing and become their child's champion."
> —Signe Whitson

Now is the time to walk through the "Classroom Door." Heck, run if you need to!

Preparing to Walk through the Door

As a parent, you do not want to walk through the "Classroom Door" with emotions running high or the intention of "bullying" the teacher into doing exactly what you want. If you walk in that way, I can tell you from a teacher's perspective that he will put up his guard; he will not listen as clearly to what you have to share, and he will go into his own fight, flight, freeze, or flee mode. You want the best outcome for your child, so first, you must calm down and get your emotions in check. I am not saying that you can't feel or be present in how you feel, but I am sharing that you can come at it with a gentle giant approach instead of like a belittling, angry lion.

Before you share, make sure you have all the facts you know about documented correctly on a piece of paper or notecard. Just in case your emotions arise (it happens to the best of us), you will have something to lean on and pull from so you do not miss bringing to light all the important pieces. The following are the facts that you will want to have and share once inside the classroom:

- Where the bullying is occurring.
- When it is happening (exact dates and times are very helpful if you know them).
- Who is bullying your child.
- What type of bullying is occurring (See "School Entrance Doors").
- How frequently it happens.
- If the teacher is present when it happens.
- What other adults are present when it is taking place.
- What your child has tried to do to stop the bullying on her own.
- How you know it is going on.

- How it is affecting your child (see "Primary Bedroom").
- If you have started counseling, you can share that and anything the counselor recommends sharing with the teacher.

Once you have all the facts written in one concise spot, take time to think about your goal or the outcome you want from this meeting. How do you want the teacher to respond? What action steps would you desire he take to stop the bullying? Are there specific consequences that should take place for the child who is bullying? (Refer to the school handbook for this one and even highlight the action they promise to take, depending on the frequency and level of bullying occurring.) How will your child feel safe again and trust the teacher in order to reenter the school? How can you work together as a team? If the bullying continues, how do you want to be notified? How should you notify the school if you discover it has recurred?

After careful thought, contact the teacher and set up an in-person meeting. This situation is *too big* for an email or text. Please honor your child and set aside time to meet one-on-one with the teacher. Each teacher has different ways they prefer to communicate with parents. Use that to set up the initial meeting. Our daughter's teacher preferred email. Therefore, we sent a general email explaining that our child was being bullied and how we desired to set up a one-on-one meeting ASAP so we could problem-solve this issue as a team. Our daughter's teacher responded quickly and understood the urgency, so a meeting was scheduled for later that week, for when it worked best for both parties.

Developing a Successful Plan

As you walk through this door prepared, know there is a good chance the teacher will do one or more of the following: deny what is going on; declare that she had no idea this was going on even if your child has tried to speak up before; put fault on someone else, such as support staff or an administrator; claim your child is just overly sensitive; or downplay it, saying they will "handle it." As a fellow teacher and parent, I have witnessed and experienced all of these responses. I am not deflating your sails as you walk through the storm. Instead, I am helping you armor up before you walk into battle.

To begin the meeting, thank the teacher for taking the time to meet with you, as you know teamwork is how this situation will be resolved. If you lead with gratitude, then hopefully your child's teacher will be open to hearing all you have to present to him and actively listen instead of put up his guard. Share the facts you have prepared but try to avoid sharing your feelings. Some feelings will arise as you share but lead with the hard facts, which the teacher cannot argue with or disprove. Explain to the teacher that the second level of Maslow's Hierarchy of Needs is not being met. Your child does not feel secure or safe when she walks through the doors. Therefore, she cannot achieve her highest level academically, socially, mentally, or physically. In addition, her basic needs of belonging and a sense of significance are being robbed day in and day out because of the bullying that is happening to her.

> **Feelings will arise but try to lead with the hard facts.**

After the facts are shared and the teacher counters or asks more questions, you need to develop an action plan together for how to resolve the bullying, as well as determine the action that will be taken if the bullying reoccurs. Depending on where, when, and how the bullying is happening, there are eight proactive solutions the teacher can take to assist your child and the student who is bullying.

The first three proactive steps require the teacher and staff at the school to work toward ensuring a *safer environment* for your child and all the other students in the classroom. First, the teacher promises to monitor the child who is bullying and "just happen" to be behind him in the space the bullying is taking place, such as in the back of the classroom, at a specific lunchroom table, in or by the bathroom, or on the playground.

Second, adults cannot stop what they do not see. So the teacher or a staff member should always be present where students convene, especially during transition times. For example, if the bullying happens in the hallway between classes or on the way to a specials class, there should always be a teacher or support staff member present for that transition.

Bullying Hot Spots:
Hallways.
Bathrooms.
Hidden places on the playground.
Locker rooms.
Entryways and exits at the school.

Third, if the bullying is happening in the classroom, an easy fix is changing the seating. The student choosing to bully should be in constant earshot of the teacher. In addition, the student receiving the bullying can switch positions in the classroom and sit by or near other children who are encouraging or compassionate.

The next four proactive steps will take a *team effort* between the teacher, student, and parent(s). You must be assertive to make sure these next steps are executed, but you can ask questions and guide the conversation gently and kindly. Ask, "How can I count on you to keep my child safe, and what is the plan for moving forward?" The teacher may take time to answer this, and honestly, you will not want a hard, fast answer because you want the teacher to consider and devise a plan he is willing to implement to bring about positive change for your child and the other students. You may need to review the previous facts you shared about the bullying. As the teacher shares the plan, I highly encourage you to write down what he shares. Then be bold enough to read back to the teacher what he promised. Once he agrees to what you reiterate, request that you both sign this plan, just like a parent would with an individual education plan (IEP) or other important legal document the school and parents agree to. I can share from personal experience that had I known about this proactive step, a lot of time and energy would have been saved on my part and a lot of heartache and headache would have been prevented for my daughter, myself, and my family. The teacher would have been positioned to be held accountable instead of the horrible back-and-forth game of "he said, she said" that unfolded.

Now that the plan is written and signed, the next action step requires more team players. If the bullying is happening when another teacher or staff member is present, that staff member needs to be made aware of the bullying and needs to buy into the plan that has been drafted. Be strong and request that all teachers or staff members who work with your child and the child who is bullying be informed of the situation(s) and the proactive steps to be taken to stop it from continuing in the future. If everyone isn't in the room, kindly inquire, "How will I know this has been shared with all the appropriate staff members? For example, will you email me once that interaction has taken place?" This step may feel uncomfortable, even weird, but I can tell you as a parent and teacher, it is imperative for the success of the action plan!

Once those steps are in place, ask, "What kind of reporting procedure would you like me to follow if I hear these problems are recurring?" Some teachers may request that the student report it to the teacher immediately when it happens so it can be addressed in real-time. Others may implement daily check-ins with the student before dismissal to make sure nothing was missed for the first couple of weeks or a month after the initial meeting. Every teacher has a different preferred mode of communication between teacher and parent: a note in the student's take-home folder, a phone call, an email, or a message in the school app where school-to-home communication is shared. Whatever is preferred, I encourage you to use that mode so that your information is shared quickly. However, I highly discourage using a note in the student's folder, as it can get lost or, if your child is older, a peer can read it and possibly take it before the teacher sees it.

The final proactive step is finding out how you will know if any action is taken against the child who is bullying. As a disclaimer, most schools and teachers will say legally, they cannot tell you the course of action they took with any other students. However, you have every legal right to be notified that the situation was addressed and how your child will be cared for if the incident happens again. This step should not be that your child will let you know. At this point, it should be the teacher's responsibility to contact you directly in the manner that works best for you both.

Take a moment to take a deep breath in and a gentle breath out. You took off your superhero cape and became superhuman. That is no small feat. Advocating for your child can sometimes be the hardest role you will take on as a parent! Through the tears, the reward on the other side can be so bittersweet for you and your child. I am going to be brutally honest, though. This probably won't be the last time you have to walk through this door. My hope for you is that you secured a positive relationship with your child's teacher, and he or she will be a stronger influence for the safety of your child at school, including inside his or her classroom. "Be the most pleasant nuisance you possibly can be until you have a resolution."[17] A good teacher will thank you for being a strong advocate for your child and partnering to create the best

> **Be the most pleasant nuisance you can be until you have a resolution."**
> **—Signe Whitson**

possible positive environment for learning, where students look forward to entering each and every day of their school year.

For those of you who feel like nothing was resolved in this room, know I see and hear you, and I feel that weight deeply. Cry, scream, pray, or do whatever you need to do to release the anger (perhaps rage) bottled up inside you. Then take a deep breath in and exhale hard to release all the fumes needing to be let out. Feel free to repeat this until you feel lighter. Now put on your boxing gloves because we are going to walk into the ring by going to the next person in the education system's chain of command: the principal or administrator. Know that the best administrators will support their teachers wholeheartedly, but the very best will also listen to you, the parent or caregiver of a precious child.

Administrator's Door

Walking through this door can seem intimidating. I am a teacher by trade, and I will be the first to share that I did not want to walk through this door. However, I knew my daughter's safety and mental state was worth this giant step.

Unfortunately, the bullying was not stopping, and I knew the next proper step was to get the administration involved. Sometimes, your child might have a good teacher, but her hands are tied by school policies and procedures. I am speaking from experience as a former teacher. I wanted only the best for my students, but sometimes, legally, I could not do what I knew needed to be done without the principal joining forces or a special team of staff members delegated to handle these bigger behavioral offenses. I even went so far as to encourage my students' parents to talk to the principal if I couldn't legally help them to get the best outcome for their child. Some teachers cower from sharing that, but I saw it as an opportunity for the parents to advocate for their children on a level I was not allowed to in my role at the school.

> **You are the one who knows what is best for your child.**

No matter the reasoning for involving the administration, you need to remember that *you* are the one who knows what is best for your child, and you should not be talked down to or told any different, no matter the title of the person with whom you are meeting—from the principal on up to the superintendent. So stand your ground and let's take that monster step or leap into the principal or administrator's office.

Before you walk through the Administrator's Door, I want to give you the best legal advice I was offered as a parent in this situation. Document and keep in a safe place every email, phone call, or in-person meeting you have with a teacher, principal, or administrator. Take notes from the meeting that outline the day and time you met, the facts and other important information discussed, the teacher's and administrator's responses, the goals or plans promised to be implemented, and dates of future proposed meetings or conversations to be held. Through this documentation, I was given a leg to stand on when teachers and administrators broke their promises because I had solid proof (in the form of documentation) about our agreement and what I was trying to uphold.

Administrators interact with many teachers, staff, parents, and students daily. Great ones will take notes, too, so they don't forget the plans and what was promised. Unfortunately, though, many administrators forget or try not to carry the responsibility of what was promised or only remember bits and pieces—sometimes only what they want to remember.

Just like you prepared for the meeting with the teacher, you will need to prepare before meeting with any administrator. The first step is to reach out to the administrator and share a brief synopsis of why you request an in-person meeting. You can meet with them online and record the meeting, but I highly suggest you meet in person. Meeting in person is more professional and shows respect for the administrator and your child. This meeting can be with the teacher also. Having the teacher present will depend on whether you feel like the teacher is the reason the bullying has not ceased, if he is truly a team player, if he is willing to bring about the change that is needed, and as long as he's not going to team up with the administrator to gang up on you.

Once the meeting is set, draft the key points you want to go over during the meeting. You will need to share the facts and answer the questions previously addressed in "Classroom Door." In addition, you will need to have the documentation you kept of the plan the teacher and you signed with the details of the discussion that took place during your meeting with the teacher. Write down any part of the plan that was not executed by the teacher and the steps you took to try to hold the teacher accountable. The last part will be important to discuss with the administrator, as he or she will want to know why you moved up the chain of command instead of just meeting with the teacher again. Finally, record what next steps you would like taken and why.

What Drives Children to Bully

One reason why the bullying may be continuing is that the teacher and staff have not taken the time to "look beyond the behavior that the child bullying is exhibiting and understand the thoughts, feelings, experiences, and perceptions that drive each child's actions."[18] There are a lot of demands on teachers, and most do not take the time to figure out the drivers for the bullying because they don't feel like they have the time. It is a lot easier for teachers to see a behavior, address it at surface level, and move on with their day. However, by not digging below the iceberg and investigating the reason for it, the

> "Look beyond the behavior the child bullying is exhibiting and understand the thoughts, feelings, experiences, and perceptions that drive each child's actions."
> —Signe Whitson

behavior will resurface and sometimes in an even more aggressive manner.

There are three main drivers for why children bully. The first is to gain social status. The old thought that kids bully because they are insecure is no longer as prevalent. Rather, children of all ages are motivated to bully to increase their social status. I saw this firsthand with my daughter. A girl who was one of her friends the previous year craved peer attention and praise. She wanted to be one of the "popular" girls. So on the playground, she sneakily implemented psychological bullying toward my daughter. The child who was bullying thought if she acted this way, the other girls would like her better and follow her lead. However, this backfired once another popular student stood up to the child who was bullying and told her she was being mean to my daughter. Then that peer went and played with my daughter instead.

A second driver for bullies is to maintain power and control. Signe shares in her book, *8 Keys to End Bullying*, "They tend to enjoy the sense of power and control they get from dominating interactions and manipulating others." This is usually seen through the "mean girl" scenario. For example, the alpha female or the peer group's "leader" exerts her power and influence in her peer group over who is considered "in" the group and who is "out" and "not allowed" to be a part of the group—for whatever reason she makes up. The other children in this group fear the alpha will turn on them, and they will be "out" of the group if they do not follow her lead. The deeper reasoning for this power to control will be discussed later in this chapter, but overall, it is usually because of feeling a lack of control in their home.

The third driver is the peer attention the child who is bullying receives. As shared in "Counselor's Office Door," all children want to feel a sense of significance and belonging. The child who is bullying others feels the same way. He wants to feel seen and have a place in the hierarchy of his social group. This can pair with the second driver in that the bully values power, control, and their social status in the hierarchy of their social group. This type of bullying escalates as the child who is bullying receives the attention he desires. Attention can be realized when bystanders laugh, peers encourage him to continue, or other students join in the bullying. Just like drugs or sugar can give a person a dopamine hit, this type of bullying gives the child who is bullying the "hit" he craves and makes his body look forward to more.

Knowing these drivers exist, parents, teachers, and administration should agree that bullying is *not* a normal part of childhood, and they should work together, using their adult influence and power, to stop the bullying from reoccurring. The only way to make the bullying stop is to dig deeper into the root cause motivating the child who is choose to bully others. The following are common factors leading to a student choosing to bully:

> **Agree bullying is not a normal part of childhood and work together using influence and power to stop the reoccurrence of bullying.**

1. Deficits in emotion management.
2. Deficits in decision-making or impulse control.
3. Deficits in attachment.
4. Deficits in belonging and significance.

A common example of this is a child who grows up in a family where anger is expressed through aggression, and he doesn't understand this is not normal. This could lead the child to physically bully a peer. He doesn't know there are better ways to handle anger. He just mimics what he sees at home.

All of these deficits lead to the phrase, "hurt people hurt people." All of the above deficits can lead to a child bullying a peer. It doesn't condone the behavior, but it can give teachers and administrators a glimpse into the root cause behind the behavior. By knowing the root cause, school professionals can come up with a better action plan for how to keep your child safe and how to guide the child who is bullying to better decisions.

Basic Types of Bullies

Once the root cause behind the behavior is solved, the next important piece is to know what type of bully is behind the behavior. I want to give another disclaimer here, though, before we dive into this concept. Despite some of the language in this book and other resources, no child should be labeled "a bully." Just like we do not want your child to carry the weight of "victim," we want to approach the child who is bullying the same way. By calling a child a "bully," we are breathing life into that title, and that is the last thing I know you want. You do not want other children to receive the same treatment your child has endured. Instead, for the remainder of this book, know that when we say "bully" we are using that word in place of the actual child's name for clarity and anonymity. However, we want the administration to team up with you, recognize the behavior in the child who is choosing to bully, and guide him to change the behavior.

> By knowing the root cause, a better action plan can be created.

> By calling a child a "bully," we are breathing life into that title, and that is the last thing we want.

The first type of bully is the "traditional" bully. This is the one we see in movies. He is big, mean, tall, and strong. He takes advantage of his stature and strength to beat up other kids, steal their stuff, and purposely hurt whoever gets in his way. This is typically the person whom a teacher and administrator thinks of when she hears the word "bully." This type was thought to have low self-esteem and a mean personality.

There is this type of student who still chooses to bully in some schools. However, research is showing that the "traditional" bully does not make up the vast majority of students who bully in schools. Instead, the "popular" bully is the most common type of bully. The popular bully is good "at reading the emotions of kids around them and manipulating them."[19] This type has a strong personality, lacks empathy for others, and exhibits a strong sense of entitlement. She instills fear in others in her group, which gives her power over them. For example, another peer worries she will not be included in the "in" group, so she follows anything the child who is bullying tells her to do. The popular child who is bullying can go as far as having other peers do their dirty work of belittling and bullying others. Thus, this type of bully is hard to pinpoint because she may not be the one engaging in the majority of the mean and hurtful behavior.

The "clueless" bully is a child who bullies without truly meaning to.[20] A common example is a child who is autistic. He may be following another peer's directions or behaviors without knowing the behavior is wrong. Or he lacks empathy for others and struggles with recognizing others' emotions, so he continues to say or do something hurtful or inappropriate, without knowing the harm it causes to the one he is doing it to.

The fourth type of bully is a "victim" bully. This category of bully tends to have psychological problems. He also has low self-esteem and a negative outlook on life. He uses what is happening to him mentally or as a victim of being bullied somewhere else to turn around and bully peers. He doesn't see himself as a bully because he has the "victim" or "poor me" mindset. Peers take turns bullying him, which causes him to, in exchange, bully another child. This type of bully can also be hot-tempered and generally irritating in the classroom.[21]

The "online" bully is the fifth category of bully. This one tends to be loud and threatening online but is meek and timid in person. She can be quiet when face-to-face with her peers then lash out online. In addition, this category of bully tends to remain anonymous online or take on a different profile name so she feels stronger in voice and stature than she is. She lacks power in real life but makes up for it in her cyber identity. Sometimes, though, this child who is bullying is loud in person, and it carries over into her online presence.

Those are the five basic types of bullies. However, not all children who show bullying behaviors fall into these cookie-cutter categories. Some bullies may have characteristics of more than one of these groups. These are the primary types that schools and counselors have identified in their countless years of working with survivors and their peers who have chosen to bully.

Being a Strong Advocate

"The mystery for adults need not be why kids bully, but rather what we can do to help them achieve a sense of belonging and significance through constructive activities and behaviors, rather than through bullying."[22] One way this can come about is by advocating for your child. You stand up for your child and say, "Enough is enough" and assertively demand, "How are you going to do better and stop making excuses for the behavior that continues to harm my child and other children down the road?" to the top leader of the school: the administrator.

You have prepared and are ready with your script. Walk through the door with your boxing gloves on. No, I do not mean bully or cause harm to the administrator. Instead, just like the best boxer who has

Your child deserves better and needs better!

prepared for the big day, put your feet to what your head and heart already know: Your child deserves better and needs *better*!

Just like you shared with the classroom teacher, explain all the facts (refer to "Classroom Door"). Remember to leave out how you feel or what you think and simply and clearly state the facts. The administrator needs to understand who is doing the bullying, what type of bullying is happening, where it takes place, when it happens, the frequency of what is happening, and why it is happening, and if the teacher or your child has figured out the root cause (that one is hard, so don't worry if you haven't solved the root cause of the bullying).

Once the facts have been shared, the next step is to share what was discussed with the classroom teacher and the plan you agreed upon. Make sure to explain how the bullying has not stopped and the plan the teacher established has not been upheld or is not working. In addition, affirm that you already contacted the teacher when the bullying situation arose again. Tell them what avenue you used to converse with the teacher and what became of those conversations. The administrator may request that you meet as a trio—administrator, teacher, and parent—to resolve this issue and develop a better plan of action.

No matter what the administrator decides, I challenge you not to let the meeting end there. Instead, pull out the school handbook. Read directly from the handbook the course of action that should be taking place as outlined in it. If that course of action is not being followed, the administrator needs to explain the reason and share what will happen after the meeting to rectify that. In addition, have them clearly define what each level of bullying looks like and the consequences to be administered for the various levels. For example, a student who physically bullies another child by punching her should not receive the same consequence as another student who passes a mean note to a peer.

After the authority figure defines each level of bullying and the consequences(s) that coincide with the offense, they should promise you how these will be implemented. For example, will the teacher notify the principal? Or will the student be sent straight to the principal's office? Additionally, the administrator should explain how the discipline and consequences will be clearly communicated to *all* students and upheld by every teacher.

Proactive Steps for Schools

Once the handbook is discussed and the proper steps are defined and discussed at great length, the next step is to agree on proactive steps the school as a whole will take to keep your child safe. This is the step I tirelessly fought for with my daughter's superintendent. She was unwilling to take easy proactive steps that would have provided safety for my child and created a positive school environment for all students who walk through the doors. One easy step is to make all staff members aware of the bullying that continues to take place. The classroom teacher is not the only adult present during the day.

> **A teacher cannot provide the best care and safety if she is unaware of what has taken place.**

For example, normally classroom teachers, paras, and support staff have different days of the week when they are assigned to supervise lunch. Until the bullying stops, all staff members who interact with your child and the student who is bullying should be monitoring both children. They should be watching to make sure your child is not being targeted and that the child who is bullying is not continuing the hurtful behavior. As a former substitute teacher, I can tell you that a teacher cannot provide the best care and safety if she is unaware of what has taken place. She may downplay an interaction if she does not know the previous trauma that has unfolded.

Another proactive step all schools can take is to identify the "hot spots" in their school. These are the places where bullying is most likely to occur, especially where there is a lack of adult supervision. The common places are hallways, bathrooms (especially starting in upper elementary and above), lunchroom, recess, locker rooms, and the bus. The administrator needs to work with all staff members to increase adult supervision in these areas, especially during transition periods. For example, when I was a substitute teacher, there would be one teacher watching up to three classrooms per grade level with the help of one or two support staff. The common classroom size was at least twenty students. That meant at least sixty students were assigned to three adults. Then add that some of the playgrounds were wide and covered a decent area from the playset to the soccer/kickball field to more open areas. On any given day, there was no way those three teachers could effectively monitor all of those areas. That was a problem.

One local school in Virginia Beach, Virginia, has troubleshooted this. They have the classrooms rotate between the various areas of the playground throughout the week. That way, the students still enjoy the entire recess area throughout the week, but the teachers can better see and hear what is going on during the allotted recess time for the students who can only play in smaller areas each day.

The third proactive step is to create safety zones in a school. These are designated areas where the children can run to if they feel threatened. This could be the counselor's office, a support staff's office, a spot by the secretary or principal's office, or others. If it is a big school building, there should be multiple safety zones so students feel getting there is not a huge feat. This is one I have not seen implemented, but I have read about success in other school systems.

An anti-bullying pledge is the fourth proactive step. This pledge is discussed and handed out at the beginning of the year to all students. They, along with their parents/guardians, are required to sign it before they are allowed to return to school. If a child or guardian refuses to sign it, then the administration needs to have a preset procedure for how to move forward. The benefit of this pledge is that the school communicates to all families that bullying is not tolerated and consequences will be administered. It upholds the child who is bullying and his guardian to the action that will be taken if the bullying occurs, and it contractually binds the school's leadership to follow the procedures it has written in its handbook. It is also a legal document you can refer to when your child is bullied.

Proper training for teachers and all school personnel is the easiest proactive step. However, it is the least activated step taken in schools. All school staff should be educated on how bullies present nowadays. Remember, most bullies are socially adept, use manipulation to get what they want, and shift the blame to the child they are victimizing while others minimize the serious problems.[23]

Another important piece for all staff members to learn is that mediation is not a proper strategy. In most bullying situations, countless counselors, bullying experts, and other authors who have thoroughly researched the topic of bullying agree that mediation puts kids of uneven power in a room together, making situations worse. "It terrifies the target and often reinforces the uneven power dynamic. It gives the bully even more information about the target and gives the bully *more* power."[24] The majority of the time mediation will make the bullying increase, which makes it worse for the victim.

> **Mediation puts kids of uneven power in a room together and "terrifies the target, often reinforcing the uneven power dynamic."**
> **—Signe Whitson**

For example, my son was bullied in fourth grade when he was the "new kid" in school. It happened at recess or during the transition to recess. The counselor used mediation, thinking it would solve the issue (this happened without my permission, and I found out afterward). My son came home that day to tell me about the meeting. Instead of helping, he informed me that the student who was bullying him called him a snitch and stupid, said other mean words, and offered him mean gestures. I quickly informed that teacher of this and requested that mediation not be the strategy used again with my child. Haber includes in his argument against mediation that "Therapists don't talk to domestic violence victims in the same room with their abusers because the power is uneven, and that rule applies with bullying incidents because there is uneven power."[25] Teachers and staff need to wake up and quit using this strategy. It is not a strategy. It is another weapon they hand to bullies when they use it.

The fifth proactive step is continuing education for all teachers and support staff on the topic of bullying. Bullying is not what it used to be in past generations. For example, cyberbullying was not happening when I was a child because Facebook, TikTok, cell phone videos, and other types of electronic platforms did not exist. This extra training can be during staff days, weekly staff meetings, conferences, book clubs, or assigned reading and reporting back when complete. This will give teachers proactive steps to take, such as the ones we previously discussed in this chapter. As a former teacher, though, I understand we do not want teachers to feel like this is an added burden. Instead, it should be offered as another effective tool in their toolbelt, helping them make strides in creating a positive school and classroom environment.

In addition to the extra training, all school staff should be well-versed in the contents of the school handbook and how things should be implemented in the school. In their initial training or orientation, when they start working for a new school or school district, teachers and staff should receive proper training in the handbook protocols they promise to uphold each day they step foot into the school. In addition, they must be kept abreast of the proper reporting and communication structure between them, the principal, the child who is bullying's parents, and the survivor's parents. All other teachers should be updated on any changes in the handbook from year to year. Additionally, if an issue continues in the school—with students or teachers not implementing consequences precisely as outlined in the handbook—this should be addressed in team, grade-level, or staff meetings. Bullying will only cease by forming a strong team between the school, the students, and their guardians, all working together to create a positive school environment.

The final proactive step is to create check-in times with the child being bullied and the child who has bullied. These should be separate meetings where the survivor and the child who is bullying are meeting with adults at different times and for different purposes. The purpose of the meeting with the survivor is to ensure no more bullying actions have occurred, ensure the student feels safe in her classroom, confirm the teacher is advocating for her as promised in "the plan," and help the survivor regulate emotions. Her meetings should be once a week at first but then taper off to once a month until she, her guardian, and the school team feel the bullying has subsided and the check-ins are no longer needed.

The child who was bullying meets with the principal or chosen staff member to keep him accountable for not repeating offenses. The initial meeting is to set the groundwork for declaring that the bullying will not be allowed to continue, outline actions that must be taken to make sure it does not happen, and understand the consequences that will be executed if the bullying continues. The focus should not be on punishing or hurting the child who is bullying, but instead have the goal of changing his behavior and hopefully changing his heart and mind toward his peers. Haber shares these effective questions that can be asked of the child who is bullying:

1. What did you do that got you in trouble? [or] Why have you been brought here for this meeting?

2. Tell me in your own words what your problem behavior was without telling anything about what the other kid did?
3. Did your behavior cross the line and hurt someone else?
4. What were you trying to get out of what you did? Attention, power, a laugh?
5. Is there another way to get what you want without hurting someone?[26]

After these starter questions, the principal will remind the child who is bullying of the anti-bullying pledge he signed. They will discuss how that contract was broken, the repercussions for breaking it, and the consequences that will be administered as outlined in the handbook. Furthermore, a thorough plan will be presented to the child who is bullying on what desired behavior is expected once he steps out of the office and what increasing consequences will be earned if the bullying continues or intensifies. Then the administrator will inform him that his parent/guardian will be notified of the behavior and the plan that has been created. The best course of action is to call the parent or guardian while the student is present. Share the facts with the parent and explain that a plan has been drafted. Then schedule a meeting with the parent, the child, the teacher, and the principal ASAP, stating it is required for the child to return to the classroom. This can be a Zoom meeting if that is the only way it can happen promptly. The best-case scenario is an in-person meeting, where non-verbal and verbal communication can be better received and everyone can sign the final action plan.

The above action steps are not an exhaustive list. Instead, they are steps that have been researched, implemented by schools, and found to be the most effective in stopping bullying. However, it takes every team member working together to bring about the positive change needed. If any of the team members cease to do their part, these will just be good ideas on a page or in an action plan.

Something all parties must remember: "When we, as adults, understand that by their very nature, kids are works in progress, and that their behavior on any given day—or even on repeated occasions—is subject to guidance and improvement, we stop placing then in harmful categories such as "bully," "troublemaker," and "problem child" and are able to view them as young people who deserve to be taught better ways to behave."[27] As the parent of the survivor, this may be a difficult quote to read let alone believe. But once you buy into the philosophy, you and your child will have a smoother healing journey, can forgive the child who was bullying, and move on in your lives (speaking from experience).

> **Adults understand that kids are works in progress and can view them as young people who deserve to be taught better ways to behave.**

Take a moment to take a deep breath in and a gentle breath out. This step can make you feel exhausted, depleted, angry, and so much more. I remember sometimes coming out of these meetings feeling like I had just beat my head against a wall, that no one truly listened or even cared. The administrator I worked with swept things under the proverbial rug, lied to my face, and ultimately was unwilling to take easy steps to better the school and keep my child safe. How could someone claim to have so much pride in her school and lead with such weakness? There is so much I could say and share here about what I felt, but it would not benefit anyone and would only belittle those who did not lead with integrity. What kept me going was you, the reader, as I knew this battle had to be won because no one should have to experience what my sweet girl and our family walked through day in and day out.

My daughter deserved better and so does yours—and so do all the generations of kids to come.

I hope a wonderful action plan was contractually signed and will be implemented by your child's school. However, I know the reality of when a school falls short of its promise. If you fall into the latter category, know this may not be the last time you enter through this door. Document everything and take courage to stand up for your sweet child.

Do not stop here! Turn the page and walk through the next door. The next door is for you, the mama (or parent/guardian). You have been through Hell and back, and now it is time to refuel and recharge!

Primary Bedroom Door

Dear sweet Mama or Dad reading this, I am so proud of you! You have become superhuman to advocate for your child, and that is no small feat. I commend you for all the time and energy you have exerted to bring light back into your child's life and help cultivate a better environment for your child in the classroom—and for the school as a whole. However, if we are being completely honest, you are exhausted at this point. Your cup is no longer full, and you probably feel like you are completely burned out . . . empty from it all.

I know this because I have been in your shoes. I remember many times walking into my bedroom, sighing a breath of relief, before wailing. You know the kind—where tears roll from the depth of your being, and you are snotty-nosed but don't even care. I had not allowed myself to feel in some of the hard daily moments because I thought if I did, my world would crumble. My child would crumble. I would collapse or explode with utter sadness, maybe even rage. All that bottled-up emotion takes a toll on our mental health and our bodies, physically, emotionally, and spiritually.

This chapter is for you. It is time for you to refuel, recharge, and breathe. You are going to take inventory of where you are as a person, not as the mama or dad, but as the human *you*. In addition, you are going to walk through the emotions you have kept in for so long, and you are going to do whatever it takes to refuel and fill yourself back up. You need to hold space for you because, honestly, no one else will. You have to love yourself and your family so much that you will take care of yourself *now*!

Circles of Influence

The first area of your life we will take inventory of is your circle of influence and your inner circle of friends or family. Here are some initial questions to consider:

- Who are you surrounding yourself with?
- Who is encouraging you?
- Who is supporting you?
- Who is still by your side?
- Who has ghosted you?
- Who is tearing you down?
- Who is questioning every decision you make and always has advice for the opposite thing you should be doing?

Some of these questions will be easy to answer, while others might be painful to reflect on.

I learned during our bullying journey who our true ride-or-die friends were. These friends check on you on any given day to make sure your head is still above water. They listen to the pain you are going through without judgment or advice, at least initially. They hold space for you when it gets too hard to do that for yourself, and they truly believe in caring for your well-being, especially your heart. Not only are these friends wanting to be by your side, but they are worried about your child. They want what is best for your child and your family as a whole. They don't judge your character because they know you on a personal level and know you would do everything in your power to garner what is best for your child—and all the other children involved.

The next group of people to consider are friends or mentors who can offer guidance and wisdom. These may be your spiritual friends, people who have a previously bullied child, adults who are further along in their parenting journey, or those who are wiser because of age, experience, or spiritual maturity. It is important that the person or people in this group avoid gossip and are willing to keep what you desire private to uphold your child's and your integrity. This group was quite small for me.

One person who fell into this group was a fellow mom whose child had gone through trauma, attended the same school, and had started to find healing with a Christian counselor. She listened to what was going on without judgment and helped me find a good-fit counselor for our daughter. That advice was a lifesaver, and she became a lifeline in this journey. In addition, she knew the true character and heart of my daughter, and she, too, wanted to bring our girl back to life again. Then, when the time came that my daughter was willing to share her story, this mom blessed us with playdates, where my daughter and hers could talk through things as they laughed, played, and did "friend things."

Besides her counselor, this friend brought the most healing for my daughter because she felt heard, seen, and valued by a peer. Slowly, she built up her courage again to be her authentic self, not what the bullies had said over her, and she could love herself again as she laid a new foundation for a strong, healthy friendship. This mom friend stayed along for the entire ride, and she checked in with me to see how my daughter and I were doing in our healing journey.

Some other mentors were ones I could ask how to properly discipline our daughter while she was in her fragile state. She still needed boundaries and rules to be upheld, but she needed more grace in how consequences were administered because her self-worth was low during this season. In addition, I needed to let a few people in when I had no more energy to parent after advocating for my child all day. They knew I was at my breaking point. They didn't judge me for being mad at times, and they intervened so I could cool off.

One of those mentors was my mom. One time, I sat at my wit's end as my daughter screamed. I wanted to scream right alongside her. Normal coping strategies that had previously worked for my daughter were not calming her down. My mom listened on the phone to what was going on then drove over to our house. She walked into the tantrum and first asked if I was okay, then hugged me and let me walk away from my daughter's tantrum. She tip-toed to my daughter's bedroom, hugged her, and calmly sat with her, listening and whispering to her. My mom let me go outside so I could yell and cry while she brought my daughter back down to the present moment where we could talk through the anger to find its source.

A third group of friends are the "confidant friends," who will encourage you and celebrate your smallest wins during this healing journey. These are the cheerleaders in your life. They are the ones who, no matter what kind of person you show up to be that day, will influence you to be the best version of yourself. They are the ones who drop you text emojis that make you laugh, Scripture that inspires you, memes that make you think, quotes that spur you on, and other treasures to make you feel seen. They are the ones you turn to during the roughest days of this healing journey. They may be your closest friends, or they may be that person who exudes joy and makes you smile just by being around them.

> **Your advocating for your child doesn't make your circle of other courageous parents shrink back but makes them want to stand up and join you.**

The fourth group of people you want in your circle of influence are the other courageous school parents. These are the parents at your child's school who are not afraid to stand up for what is right. Your advocating for your child doesn't make them shrink back but makes them want to stand up and join you. This may be parents of your child's friends, or it may be other families currently walking the same bullying road as you (or have in the past). This group is harder to find because many parents like to hide in privacy or run away from confrontation instead of walking the hard road of being an ambassador for positive change in the school. Many people are waiting for the first courageous parent to stand up, but they are scared to be that parent. Sometimes all it takes is one parent standing up to start a ripple of other parents banding together. This is what I saw in my experience. Initially, I had no one by my side, and it was a lonely path to walk. However, once I became a "spokesperson" for my daughter—and all of the students who seemed just as voiceless—other parents slowly shared their children's stories, and a few started voicing their concerns to teachers and the administration.

> **Sometimes all it takes is one parent standing up to start a ripple of other parents banding together.**

Unfriending

Now that we have discussed who to keep in your friend network, we need to touch on the types of people you may need to release, or throw up a few extra boundaries around. The first group comprises those who say your child brought the bullying on herself, that she deserved it, or that she needs to buck up because it is "just a part of childhood." This group will not be in your or your child's corner. And honestly, if you surround yourself with this group of people, you are going to wear yourself down and look at your child in a negative light. You do not need to add salt to your open wounds or stress or psychological negativity to your days. Walking the road of healing through bullying is consuming in itself, and you need people who are going to uplift and fill you, not tear you down.

The next group of people you need to stop being around—or at least take a break from—is the group that gossips about you or your child. The woman who wants to know everything that is going on, but then, once you walk away, she shares all of "your business" with whoever crosses her path next. She shares all the intimate details of your journey that were meant only for her. She is the one who thinks everyone's story is hers to share. Our story is "our story," and without permission, no one else should be sharing it with the world. These might also be the people who point at your child when she walks into a room or who start whispering to the other ladies around you. Even if she tells you she is just helping, know she is *not* helping anyone! She is slandering you and spreading your story to any listening ear. That is not a friend.

The final friend group you need to consider is composed of those who have ghosted you or no longer talk to you. These are the women who have said they are your friends, but now that you are speaking up to the teachers and administration, they pretend you no longer exist. For example, you walk into the school, and these people pretend they do not see you or quickly look busy or walk in the opposite direction. Or these are the ones who no longer return your calls, texts, or messages. There may be many reasons why these people are like that now. However, the overarching reason for most is that you have now spoken out against school authorities, and they do not want to be acquainted with you for fear of retaliation or rejection. They do not want to be seen as someone who goes against authority. Instead of asking all the questions about why they are not speaking to you, you need to accept what has happened and know deep down they were not "friends" in the first place. They are not strong people, and you don't want to spend your precious time and energy on them. That may sound harsh. But I can tell you from experience, at the end of the day, you have to save whatever energy you have for you and your family, and for getting light back into your child's life.

Time to Refuel

Now that you know who is and who is not on your side, it is time to refuel, recharge, and fill your cup again. After this journey with your child, it may be hard to even think about what will light the fire inside you again, but you need to! Self-care is a buzzword these days, but let's start there. What relaxes you? A bubble bath? Lit candles with piano music? A charcoal mask? A pedicure while sitting in a massage chair? Worship music blaring for you to sing and dance to? Snuggling up in a chair with a warm blanket and a book? Prayer, a journal, and a pen? A cup of tea in your hand and a podcast playing in your headphones? A walk or a run with a gentle breeze in your face? Hitting a volleyball or tennis ball, or punching a boxing bag? What is something you can do by yourself to be yourself again? This does not have to be something that costs money, but it should be time well spent, alone, to relax and calm your body from all the stresses it has taken on recently. This is not a one-time-and-done thing. You will need to come back to these self-care ideas to rejuvenate your mind, body, and soul throughout this healing journey.

> **What is something you can do by yourself to be yourself again?**

After you have had time alone, I challenge you to find time to get away with a friend. This can be a one-hour coffee date once a month, a jog through the park, a tennis match, or a movie night at a friend's house. I challenge you to make this time away from your home.

Walking into your home causes you to pick it all back up, and this is time for you to lay it all down at your front door and breathe. This is time with a friend to talk about what is going on, but most of all, it is time for you to no longer be Mom, superhuman fighter, or defender. Instead, it is time to be *you* and feel happy again. A big challenge for you might be not talking much about your current journey but instead dreaming again, laughing again, playing again, and making new memories that will stretch your brain and rewire it for fun again!

Once you have alone time and friend time, I am going to push you one step further. When you feel like your child who has been bullied is in a better mindset, find a night or weekend where you can slip away. This can be a girls' weekend with friends, a spiritual retreat, or time away to pursue a passion. One of the most healing things for me was a weekend away, where I looked inward and upward and dreamed again. I attended a women's event where I was filled up and offered space to hope again, and where the idea of this book was cried over and birthed! It was the best choice I made for myself in our healing journey because, at that point, I was burned out—depleted. I had truly lost track of who I was, what it meant to dream, and what it felt like to be hopeful again. Once again, this doesn't have to cost a lot of money or require an airplane to get to the destination (but it could). This is time for *you* to be *you* and find *you* again!

Showing Up for Other Children

If you have multiple children, this next part is for you. It is a difficult balancing act, trying to build your child who has been bullied up while also being Mom to the other child or children. I am a mama of four, so I can tell you from experience that this is a juggling act, for sure. My daughter who was bullied initially took her anger out on her siblings. This was not only heartbreaking for me to see, but it was mentally draining and broke my heart for her brothers who had to endure her actions and words. By the time I had assisted her in calming down, I had no energy for my boys. They wanted to play outside with Mom, and all I wanted to do was curl up in a ball with a book, Netflix, or my pillow and make it all go away once my husband walked in the door. However, this would not have been a healthy or lasting strategy for me, day in and day out, and it definitely would have alienated my other children and hurt our relationship.

Initially, you may need to do the above to survive in the beginning stages of your child's healing journey. As the days go on, find five or ten minutes a day where you can be with your other child(ren). Each child is unique, and time with you can look different and take on various forms of energy. One of my boys wanted to spend outdoor playtime with me. His heart was content throwing the football in the front yard while telling me about his day. Another one of my boys wanted to snuggle next to me and read a book, play cards, or play a board game. He didn't need to talk very much; he just needed time with me present next to him. My third son was younger, so he often requested I hold him, rock him, read a book to him, or something that required my time and physical touch. By giving your children this time, you remind them that they are special, worthy of your time and energy, and loved by you.

Another fun idea with your other children is to have a mother-daughter or mother-son date. This can be fifteen minutes to hours long, depending on your time and the availability of someone who can watch your other children. Take him to get an ice cream cone. Go to the nearest park and race down all the slides together. Drive to a soccer field and kick the soccer ball around. Go to a cheap restaurant and order a meal, or better yet, treat him to his dessert of choice. I had one boy who requested we spend the morning garage sale hunting. It doesn't have to be giving him the world, but your time means the world to him.

> **Your time means the world to all your children.**

Looking back on my daughter's healing journey, this is something I would do differently. I would purposely set aside more time to pour into my other children. I took all my time and energy and poured them into my daughter, which she needed, but my mama heart needed the time away to laugh and play with my other children too. But it wasn't just for me. They really needed that undivided attention and love, especially during the beginning season of healing, when the home environment was not a positive place to be once big sister walked in the door. We had become her safe zone, but it felt rocky for all the others.

Your Childhood Trauma

We have touched on how you can refuel and how you can pour into the rest of your family. There is another topic I must touch on before we go through the next door. That topic is *your* childhood trauma. As you navigate your child's emotions, it will bring up emotions inside of you that you may have not experienced in a long time. You could have come from a loving family home, but every child goes through hurts even with the best family environment.

One emotion that often came up for me was anger. It would take me back to moments in my childhood when I did not feel seen, heard, or valued. In addition, it reminded me of when I was misunderstood. Flashbacks of names and labels people spoke over me like "hot-tempered redhead," "very emotional," "out of control," "spitfire," "too much," "loud mouth," "never shuts up"—the list could go on and on. I thought I had moved past all of that, but it's eye-opening to discover the inner child that comes out in our minds when our children walk through their trauma.

> **It's eye-opening to discover the inner child that comes out in our minds when our children walk through their trauma.**

Another common thing that arose for me was fear—fear that my daughter would turn into a mean-hearted child. I felt that anxiety in my body whenever she erupted. I saw her spewing her frustration at home, especially with her siblings, and I feared she would never change and this would spill over into her time at school. I had neither heard about the iceberg analogy ("Home Front Door") nor talked through this with my daughter's counselor yet. When my daughter's big emotions would gush out, I could feel my blood pressure rising and a tightness in my chest and shoulders. It took practice for me to walk away from her during those inciting moments and go to another room, usually my bedroom, so my emotions and reactions would not match what she was feeling at that moment.

When your childhood trauma comes to the surface, I encourage you to avoid stuffing it back down. There is a reason it is resurfacing, and you need to let it escape in a healthy manner. Instead of stuffing it, recognize it and name it. Then figure out where it is coming from and how you can work through it. The best way I worked through this was by voicing it to my daughter's counselor. She specialized in trauma-centered counseling, and she helped me understand how our children's trauma can trigger the past hurt and trauma we experienced and bring it to the light, especially if we never dealt with it. She helped me take an internal survey of where it was coming from, where I felt it in my body, and how I could release it in a healthy manner. We do not want our past traumas to place more fear, big emotions, or unhealthy reactions on our children as they work through their trauma. It is a *normal* brain reaction for your past traumas to be

> **We do not want our past traumas to place more fear, big emotions, or unhealthy reactions on our children as they work through their trauma.**

triggered and brought to recollection while your child is working through her journey and exhibiting extreme emotions during her healing.

Another way I dealt with my childhood trauma was by talking it out with my ride-or-die friends. Remember, these are the friends who will listen first, well before offering advice, and do not judge you for your actions or feelings. They are people who will not gossip to others about what you share with them in private. I texted, messaged, or called these friends when these emotions surfaced. They knew me well enough to know I was a kind-hearted person and that something inside of me was triggered and needed to be worked through. These friends were also not afraid to speak the truth in love over me and call me out when I made a mistake or was not in a positive mindset. They would bring me back to the present moment and ground me in the truth they knew about me. In addition, they were willing to pray for me, encourage me, and check up on me to make sure my mind cleared and got back on track. They weren't there to pass judgment, blame, or shame me. Instead, they were there to call out the truth about me in those hard moments and help me sift through memories and emotions to heal the past hurt spoken over me or my child—and to minimize the fears I harbored about our future, particularly my daughter's.

If you are feeling stuck in a thought, fear, or truth that isn't reality, I highly encourage you to reach out to that friend who is wiser or further along in her healing journey. She can look back on her journey and share how she overcame that big emotion or the lie that seemed so truth-filled in the moment. In addition, she knows you well enough to know your true character, your child's personality and character, what makes you both tick, and what has helped you in the past. If she is your wise mentor, you have spent time with her, building a relationship and trust between you both. This mentor knows your strengths and weaknesses, and she can tap into those to help you navigate whatever untruth is still swirling in your head. However, this wise friend may also suggest you seek out a counselor for yourself.

This bullying journey is not just affecting all aspects of your child's life, but it is consuming yours too. It is okay—even highly encouraged—to seek out a professional who will listen to you and offer strategies to call out the dark lies and ease the mental load engulfing your life, especially inside your mind. Instead of seeing this as a weakness, know that it takes loads of strength to seek out another individual or professional to bring to light what is going on internally, to excavate whatever is holding you back and replace it with truth and love for yourself.

Your Spiritual Well-Being

I would do a disservice to you, the reader, if I didn't close out this chapter with this important topic of spiritual well-being. It is imperative you make time for your spiritual well-being. I know bullying is not just a battle between one human and another. If you believe in Jesus, you know that every day, hour, minute, and second, there is a spiritual battle happening between good and evil.

Bullying, at its roots, is the enemy creating division and destruction among people. The enemy is out to steal your child's identity, kill her worth and value by making her feel insignificant, destroy the truth she believes about herself, and make her believe she doesn't belong. As I sit here and write, I have a sticky note attached to my writing binder that says, "Enemy wants to kill, steal, and destroy." This is my reminder of why I sit here, writing this book for *you*!

> **Every day, hour, minute, and second, there is a spiritual battle happening between good and evil.**

Every person was placed on this earth for a purpose. The enemy wants us so stuck that we forget that purpose and do not walk out the mission we have been called to. So it is crucial we lean into the Source of Life. Take time to sit quietly with Him. That can be five or ten minutes of stillness as you listen to His voice—or just listen to what He has created around you to get you grounded again. There is so much noise and distraction in our lives that we need to be still to find inner peace before going about our day.

Another way to tap into the Life Source is by opening your Bible. There is no right or wrong place to start when reading the Bible. The most important thing is to open it up, read it, and let it fill your mind with truth about your life. So many lies have been spoken over your child—and maybe even you—therefore, you need to replace those lies with truth that will penetrate your heart and soul.

Third, find at least one Scripture a week to memorize and rewire your brain with it. Scientific research shows that as we engage our brains, like we do while memorizing Scripture, we are stimulating neurons to rewire those parts that have been broken, and we are storing this truth in our minds for later use as well.

> **Many lies have been spoken over your child (and you); therefore, you must replace those lies with truth.**

Fourth, I encourage you to play, sing along, and dance to worship music. When we lead with praise, even before we get the result we hope for, we are opening up our minds to the positive and letting God infuse every part of us. We are shifting our focus from our current circumstances, and we are centering ourselves on His power, His faithfulness, and His strength to help us through.

The final thing I encourage you to do is to pray and cry out to God. He is waiting for us to hand over our burdens to Him. They were never ours to carry and bear. Matthew 11:28–30 states, "Come to me, all who are weary and burdened, and I will give you *rest*. Take my yoke upon you and *learn* from me, for I am gentle and humble in heart, and you will find *rest* for your souls. For my yoke is easy and my burden is light" (emphasis mine). We need to learn to rest in Him. I am not talking about lying down and sleeping (even though you may need that too). Instead, I am explaining your need to sit at His feet, weep when you need to weep, scream when you need to release the anger and pain, share your fears of the unknown and your future, talk to and with Him, and let Him take all your emotions and fears and release them, trading them for hope and joy.

Jennie Allen shares in her book, *Untangle Your Emotions*, "God made us to feel, created it all inside us. So, emotions can't be evil. They must be good *gifts* if God feels them and built them for us . . . emotions are not meant to control us; they are meant to *inform* us. To *alert* us. To *connect* us. To *remind* us that we're alive and to *help* us make sense of the world around *us* (emphasis mine).[28]

> **Emotions are not meant to control us; they are meant to inform, alert, connect, and remind us we are alive—and to help us make sense of the world around us.**

By going to God, He will help you uncover the meaning behind your emotions and direct your path on what next steps to take. Author Jennie Allen additionally suggests, "We think God is waiting for us to pull ourselves together, but actually, He is waiting for us to come to Him and fall apart. The more I do this, the more I heal."[29] Sweet parent, take off your parent cape, take on your child-like character, and fall into Him and His healing, grace-filled, gentle hands.

Take a moment to take a deep breath in and a gentle breath out. Give yourself a giant hug and scream a loud WAHOO! You have just held space for yourself! You have reminded yourself that you are special, valued, and worthy of your time to refuel, recharge, and refill your innermost being. Throughout this journey, step back into this room when you need to rest and replenish. I would love to say this door is a one-time entrance, but I can tell you from experience, I needed to step back through this door more times than I can count. Working through trauma is the most challenging work you and your child will do, and some days, it is the most draining part of walking through this world. Remember that your emotions inform, alert, and connect you to others and to God, and remind yourself of this: If you still have breath in your lungs, you need help. Please do not stuff and suppress these emotions as they rise and fall. Walk back into this room. Let them out. Navigate them and discover their purpose in your body and mind. But never stay stuck in those emotions. Let them rise over you like a wave but then crash and dissipate. Those emotions are never meant to bury you and keep you down. They are meant to alert you, so walk through them, and connect you with yourself, others, and God. Walk in the freedom of releasing your emotions and feel life again. The good life that was meant to remain hopeful and joy-filled!

Child's Bedroom Door

The "Primary Bedroom Door" is where you fill yourself back up and are reminded of your worth, value, and purpose. The child's bedroom is where you will strengthen your child by reclaiming her significance, belonging, strength, and voice again. She has been so torn down by the lies spoken over her, but now is the time she takes back rightful ownership of her life and truth.

Every child's bedroom should be her sacred place in the house, and we want to keep it that way. We don't want it to be a place where she recollects all of the horrible emotions of bullying. Instead, we want her bedroom to be her safe haven, a place where she can let it all out, restore her identity, and heal from all that has been placed on her, over which she had no control. It will be imperative that you intervene in this room *with* her, and you walk through the door gently whenever you enter here. She has to be ready to let you in, not forced to share or feel anything she is not ready for. You, as the parent, need to follow her lead as you navigate emotions, remember the trauma she has endured, and reclaim her joy and pride in who she is and will be.

Bedtime Chats

As a parent and childhood educator, I have learned that bedtime is the time when most children's (and parents') brains replay what happened in their day. This is the best time to sit or lie beside them and listen. For my daughter, this was the key time that let me to understand what was really happening. It helped me realize she was being bullied (and the severity of it) and where we reconnected and rebuilt our relationship.

Bullying survivor and teen author Aija Mayrock describes the inner turmoil children face at bedtime: "The haunting is the never-ending, rapid speed at which your thoughts pick at and attack your mind throughout the entire day. It is the constant going over and over and over everything you said, did, heard, felt, saw—it is the endless attack that is bullying. Even when people aren't bullying you, their past attacks are haunting you."[30] The good news is you can intervene in this "haunting," and you can help your child rewrite the narrative she plays inside her mind.

The best way to intervene is to have daily check-ins with your child, especially at bedtime. You can ask the following questions:

1. What was your favorite part of your day? How did that make you feel and why?
2. What feeling do you get when you think about your day?
3. What part of your day was challenging?
4. Was there a time you felt hurt, mad, sad, or something else?—it is important to note that a child should only tell their trauma once, so once she has shared, don't make her elaborate more than she wants to.
5. Did you share that feeling with your teacher?
6. Who did you play with today?
7. What did you do at recess, lunch, or specials?
8. Did you feel safe at school today? Why or why not?
9. Is there anything you really want me to know about your day?
10. Is there anything you didn't share with your teacher that you want me to hear?

This should not be a drill session. If it feels like one, then stop asking questions. Always let your child lead. The most important part of this is two-fold. First, you want to build trust between you and your child so she knows she can share anything and everything with you. She needs to know you will not judge her but, instead, will be a strong advocate for her. The second important part of bedtime talks is to help your child release her emotions, frustrations, and pain so they don't overtake her and leave her feeling hopeless—and sleepless.

When you first start this practice, especially if it is not something you have done in the past, it may just be you lying or sitting with your child. Your presence next to her may be all she needs initially. You being fully present reminds her she is worthy of others and their time, and that her life is significant, as you are taking time to be with her at that moment. Words may not come out for a while because she has stuffed them down and numbed them in her body. However, a simple hug, a hand on her leg, a hand clasped with hers, or your physical body and warmth lying next to her may remind her she is alive and that someone cares about her. Think about your life; sometimes you do not want to talk, but just having someone in the room near you makes you feel better in the moment.

Once you have made bedtime chats a part of your bedtime routine, you will not have to ask as many questions. For my daughter, all I had to do was lie down next to her and say, "Tell me about your day." Over time, everything spilled out. Sometimes I would get busy with her brothers' needs, and she would ask, "Hey, Mom, are you going to lie next to me tonight?" This became her outlet, and she knew how important and needed it was for her day and her sleep.

Some people may ask, "Well, aren't you coddling them? Aren't you enabling them?" My response is when your child is a teenager,

> **Bedtime talks release emotions, frustrations, and pain so they don't overtake her and leave her feeling hopeless.**

do you want them to naturally connect and talk to you about her day? Do you want it to be a normal routine to come to you with the big and small things? Or do you want to have to start over and beg your way back into her life when she is a teenager, which will feel like pushing a boulder up a hill? Humans are made for community and connection. You get to help her decide who to let in, who to trust, and who might add value to her life.

These bedtime chats help your child release her fears, worries, and emotions to you. It allows her to bring them all to light, with the light switch turned on. Once the lights go off and she falls asleep, we do not want lies, negative feelings, or memories to replay in her mind and carry over into her dreams—or worse, into nightmares. However, as you allow her to release her fears and emotions day after day, those events and feelings will no longer have a hold on her mind and her subconscious because new, positive thoughts and truth will replace them, as will be discussed in more detail in this chapter and the next.

> **Humans were made for community and connection. You get to help your child decide who to let in, who to trust, and who might add value to her life.**

Daily Check-Ins

Just like the bedtime chats, daily check-ins are an important part of the healing process. Initially, you will want to reach out daily, but as your child heals, it will become less and less frequent. You are gauging the barometer of your child as she enters the home. For my daughter, this check-in happened differently each day. Initially, I picked her up from school and asked, "How was your day?" On the very hard days, her nonverbals, and sometimes her verbal response, let me know her day had been challenging, and it would be better addressed in confidence at home, away from her siblings. Other times, she would tell me as we drove out of the school parking lot what emotion arose when she thought of her day and how it went.

Just like with the bedtime talks, this should be led by your child, and she should not be bombarded with questions. Some days, I didn't even need to ask how the day went because her nonverbals told me everything. For example, if she stepped into the car with huffing and puffing and a scowl, I knew at least one part of her day had been challenging, and we needed to unpack it once she was calmer.

The same questions discussed in the "Bedtime Chats" can be used during the daily check-ins. Although, there are a couple of differences between the bedtime chats and the daily check-ins. First, the daily check-ins give you a quick gauge of how your child might enter your home or if an after-school activity is a good idea. If your child is sad or mad, then you are not going to want to take her to the school playground, the park, or a playdate because that wouldn't be what is best for her or the others around her. Second, these check-ins help you understand if your child needs quiet time alone to decompress before doing anything with the rest of the family or friends. Third, it makes you aware of the calming and coping strategies she will need to work through once she is in the safety of your home. Next, it helps you validate her emotions after you help her recognize the emotion and name it. For example, "I am sad because _____ did not let me play with my group of friends at recess. I am mad and embarrassed because _____ said mean things about me at PE, pointed at me, and laughed."

Finally, it prepares your body and checks your emotions for the next steps ahead, for when she enters your home. It helps you mentally prepare for the challenges that may open up as she walks into her safe zone.

Coping Strategies

Once your child has checked in with you and recognized and named her emotion, she needs to choose a coping strategy she has already practiced. It is very important that you talk about and practice this when she is calm because, in the heat of the moment, she is not going to be using her "thinking brain." The following coping strategies are ones you can discuss with her and have her practice during those times she feels an emotion on a lower level or when she is calm:

1. Deep belly breaths. Deep breath in and "lion breath" out, "Hahhhh!"
2. Stop and scream, saying, "It's not my fault! I don't deserve this!"
3. Place bubble wrap on the floor and stomp on it.
4. Lie on your back and kick your legs in the air.
5. Talk to an adult about your feelings.
6. Journal your feelings and frustrations.
7. Relax in a bath or shower.
8. Play calming or worship music.
9. Exercise—go for a walk or a run.
10. Shoot hoops with a basketball or kick a soccer ball into a net.
11. Read a book.
12. Pray, read a devotional, read the Bible, or fill back up spiritually in some other way.
13. Pick a hobby you can do individually, away from others (e.g., scrapbook, take pictures, make jewelry, sew, paint, draw, etc.).

This is not an exhaustive list, but these are researched coping strategies that counselors and other professionals have had children successfully implement. It helped the children work through their emotions and get back into their thinking brains. Not all of these will work for your child. So it is important to share them with her slowly, letting her decide what works for her. She may have to try each one to determine what works for her. Disclaimer: Some of the ones that work for me—and I thought would work for my daughter—made her behavior escalate. That is why you both must be flexible when trying these out; allow her to change her mind and experiment with different ones. If something is not on this list but works to calm your child down, then as long as it is safe, have her do that instead.

Shedding Light on a Child's Day

Once your child has chosen a coping strategy or two, she can come back to her thinking brain and work through what happened with you. Remember, you can ask the questions discussed in "Bedtime Chats." The important piece is to figure out where the big emotion stemmed from and help her talk through the situation that happened. We always want to bring the situation to light instead of having our child keep it stuffed down and suppressed until a later time, when it's sure to explode out. Ensure your child feels seen and heard. Do not put words in her mouth; instead, ask probing questions if you are not getting the whole picture. Here are some of the most important questions to dive deeper and find the root of the emotion:

1. When in your day did you feel _____? [Say the emotion they showed when they entered your vehicle or house.]
2. What happened before that feeling?
3. What happened after you felt that way?
4. Why did that make you feel that way?
5. Did you share that feeling with your teacher? Why or why not?
6. What did the teacher or staff member do after you shared?
7. Do you feel the situation was resolved?

8. How could we make sure that doesn't happen again? What could the teacher, you, or me do instead?
9. Do you feel safe to go back to school? If not, then what would make you feel safe again?

If your child does not have the mental capacity or the energy to walk through these steps, give her space to just *be*. You can circle back at bedtime. Some days are more traumatizing and draining than others. On those days, you need to pour into your child. Fill her back up. Help her feel a sense of belonging and significance and be present when she is ready to talk about anything. Sometimes, the best thing for your child as she is healing is to encourage her to get away from all the noise of the day and do something that makes her feel unique (i.e., special) or that she likes to do, such as painting, drawing, creating something, shooting hoops, cooking, baking, etc. As long as she is not in a negative state mentally, let her lead you in if she wants to talk and open up—and follow her lead if she wants to be alone or do something quietly alongside you. There is no right or wrong method here as long as you allow her to work through everything and continue to heal.

If your child opens up and shares answers to the above questions, then let her know how proud you are of her for opening up and showing bravery by sharing what happened and how she felt. After she has answered all the questions, determine if everything was resolved, if she is safe to return to school, and if she has support at school. While thinking through those things, if the answer is no to one or more, walk back through the "Classroom Door" or "Administrator's Door," depending on the plan you agreed on with the school. As shared in those chapters, you may need to walk through those doors more than once, but know that your child will thank you for advocating for her. I can share from experience . . . I honestly lost track of how many times I had to walk through those doors, and I only know the number because of the data I kept. However, I would walk through those doors all over again the same number of times if my daughter needed me to and it allowed her to heal better knowing that I was relentless for her mental, physical, emotional, psychological, and spiritual health.

Take a moment and take a deep breath in and a gentle breath out. You have entered your child's special room, her bedroom. This is her landing area, her sacred room that she gets to call her own. You have helped her regain her strength and voice. She has confided in you what has been going on internally and externally while at school as we caught a glimpse of her mind in "The Attic." She has trusted you with her hardest moments, and that is a big feat in itself. She feels seen, heard, and valued enough to bring it to light in the hope of zero judgment or pain to come from the release. You are helping her believe she is significant and belongs again. That is what every child and adult desires. Take a mental picture of this moment because your child (and possibly you) now has hope to help her see she is a survivor, not a victim. She will get through, and she will come out stronger on the other side as long as you continue to heal together.

Please keep in mind that you will need to walk through this door daily until your child no longer answers "no" to the following two questions and no longer feels bullied:

1. Do you think the situation was resolved?
2. Do you feel safe to go back to school?

Also remember that as you walk through this door, you will need to keep walking through the "Counselor's Door" to acquire more strategies to rewire your child's brain to believe the truth over her life, not the lies spoken over her. That should not feel like defeat. Instead, you should feel hopeful that you have made it to this point. You are on the way to getting your child back again. Your joy-filled, smiley, and ready-to-conquer-the-world child.

Child's Bathroom Door

Your child and you walked through her bedroom door so that she could regain her voice, strength, significance, and belonging. Now she will be walking through the "Child's Bathroom Door" daily to rebuild her worth, value, and identity. The child who was bullying her has stripped her of her identity, and we are here to reclaim it. Teen author and bully survivor Mayrock states in her book, "It isn't easy to leave bullying in the past when being bullied is such a part of your present. You will see that you have to let go of your pain and your past to become the Real You and start a new phase of your life."[31]

Now is the time to start that new phase, and hopefully, your child is ready to jump through this door. Releasing that part of the year can be emotional and painful for your child, but it is worth it—and it's time to scream like a warrior, "LET'S GO!" It is battle time! You are not battling the child who is bullying at this moment; instead, you are taking back what is rightfully your child's: her *true* value, worth, and most of all her *identity*!

> It's time to take back what is rightfully your child's: her true value, her worth, and her identity!

Facing Fears

The first step to reclaiming worth is for your child to face the fears that come up when she thinks of being bullied again. Have her write out all of her fears and talk through what each of those fears are, how they make her feel, and why she is still holding on to them. This may be too hard for younger children, so change the language or have her draw or paint a picture of her fears or emotions each day instead of talking through them. Then have her practice something positive to replace those fears with when they arise. Here are examples of positive ways to work through fears:

1. Draw or paint a picture of the feeling.
2. Write or journal the fear, how it feels, and how to overcome it.
3. Talk to a counselor or trusted adult.
4. Exercise or play a desired sport.
5. Cook or bake.
6. Sing and dance to a favorite worship song or upbeat music with positive lyrics.
7. Read a book.
8. Go outside and play, walk, run, or bike.
9. Play with an animal (i.e., a pet).
10. Pick one thing she likes or loves to focus on for thirty minutes to one hour.
11. Pray, meditate, read a devotional, read the Bible, or do something spiritual to fill herself back up.
12. Act out the fear and how it will end positively.
13. Take a warm shower or bubble bath.
14. Take a nap.
15. Jump in puddles, throw snowballs, or something similar to release the fear outdoors.

Battle Plan

Once your child's fears have been brought to light and released, it is time for her to create her battlefield scenarios and build her "battle plan," as coined by teen survivor Aija Mayrock.[32] This is an activity for upper elementary students and older. Parents can simplify this for younger children, but a lot of the mental load in this activity will be carried by the parents of young students. The older child will need to think through all the places she goes in her school day and the people she encounters in those spaces. She will create a battle plan for all the locations where she has been bullied. Have her begin with whichever one causes her the least anxiety, and then have her work up to the area where the most frequent bullying occurred.

Now, thinking of that first place, she will work through the "4 Ps." Mayrock coins it the "5 Ps," but for this book, we're going to focus on four of them. The first P is *People*. Who are the usual people in this area? Who does she talk to? Who talks to her? Who does she pass? Who are the safe people—her allies and friends? Who is the person or people who are challenging her safety and bullying her?

The second P is *Place*. She needs to visualize that place and find an escape route if she is bullied there. She names it. Mentally practices walking through the escape route to safety. Is it the nearest teacher's classroom? The nurse's office? Or is it a safe zone her teacher or the administration designated for her, or anyone else who needs safety?

Partner is the third P. This is a friend, teacher, or staff member who is her ally in that area. Is it the reading specialist? The speech teacher? The counselor? Her friend who always stands up for her or for what is right? Is it an older student? Sometimes, the parent or teacher needs to intervene here to distinguish who a "partner" is in that area. Bullying takes its toll, and it can feel like everyone is against her. The parent needs to build the child back up and help her see there are allies all around.

The fourth P is *Path*. The child should think through every trail to her destination and choose the one that is safest for her. For example, if she is a middle school student, she will be switching classes. If there are two hallways to her next class, she might need to pick the longer one that will take more time because there are more adults in that hallway. An elementary student example might come with lining up on the playground to go into the building after recess. She needs to think of where the adults or her "partners" are and make sure she walks that path to lining up.

Your child will repeat the 4 Ps for all the sites where she has been bullied. This does not have to be completed in one sitting. It may be exhausting for the child, especially if she is younger. Be willing to make battle plans throughout the week when your child is alert and ready to warrior up. Once the battle plans are drafted, have her practice them one at a time in the safety of your home. She can act out the scenarios with her stuffed animals, Barbies, action figures, or anything else. She may notice, as she is acting out a plan, that there is a better solution and things can be tweaked. Once she has practiced the battle plan and is confident with it, she will be ready to put the battle plan into full effect and come out the victor.

Spoken Truth: I AM Statements

The physical battle plan has been drafted for when your child is in school. Now she needs to address her mental battlefield, her mind. Lies have been nonverbally, verbally, and possibly physically hurled all over her. She needs to unpack the lies her mind captured, believes, and plays on autopilot even after her season of bullying. Some of these will have become so ingrained that they will be hard to excavate, throw out, and replace with the truth of who she really is. The first step in this process is to identify those lies. An easy way to do this is by writing them down and releasing them through spoken

> **Your child needs to unpack the lies her mind captured, believes, and plays on autopilot.**

language. Her mind has wrapped itself so hard around these false beliefs that the root cause may be difficult to find. However, the goal is to uproot the lies, so she will need to push through the pain of the lie and discover where it came from to become victorious on the other side. I challenge you to ask her to partner with you in this; do this activity together. It is so much easier to release a lie when someone is next to you, acknowledging the lie, dispelling it, and speaking truth in place of it.

We are going to walk through the basic process of how to replace a lie with the truth, of how she can speak encouragement over herself daily. For those who are spiritual, we are going to pair it with scriptural truth to make the words more believable, heartfelt, actionable, and *power*-full! Here are the five steps to follow for replacing lies with truth:

1. Identify the lie.
2. Recall who spoke the lie over her.
3. Recognize where the lie was spoken.
4. Replace the lie with truth.
5. Match the truth with Scripture for *power*.

For example, let's say, "I am stupid" is the lie. —> A classmate called her stupid when playing basketball at recess when she missed a basket. Then no one wanted to play with her —> The truth is **I am smart/I have been chosen.** "But you are a chosen people, a royal priesthood, a holy nation, God's special possession, that you may declare the praises of him who called you out of darkness into his wonderful light" (1 Peter 2:9). God only makes masterpieces who are special and chosen, not dumb people!

Your child must walk through all five steps with each lie that has taken over her mind. Here are the most common lies people believe after being bullied, but a more exhaustive list can be found and printed off through the QR code at the back of this book:

- I am stupid —> I am smart (Psalm 139:14).
- I am weak —> I am strong (Isaiah 40:30–31).
- I am worthless —> I am worthy/precious (Proverbs 31:10).
- I am not loved —> I am loved (Romans 8:38).
- I am ugly —> I am beautiful (Song of Solomon 4:7).

Once time has been spent recognizing the lies that have been deeply rooted in your child's mind, the time has come to rewire her brain. She will choose one of the truths and write it on a notecard, sticky note, or piece of paper. Next, she will tape it to her bathroom mirror, where her eyes will see it every day. Each morning, as she brushes her hair, brushes her teeth, and looks at herself in the mirror, she will say the new truth out loud and recite the Bible verse that matches it. For example, while looking in the mirror, she says, "I am beautiful! *You are altogether beautiful, my love* (Song of Solomon 4:7)." This will help fire neurons in her brain and rewire her brain to think of the truth over the lie. As she looks in the mirror and says this, she speaks truth over herself and reclaims her new identity. She can practice this first truth for at least one week. Remember, the lie took time to develop roots in her brain, and the uprooting and refilling process may take a week or longer, depending on how often her brain has replayed it in the past.

As the first truth becomes second nature, your child will add another truth to the mirror—and continue adding each new truth to her routine until all the truths are spoken over her and the lies are uprooted and released from her body. Additionally, you can take it a step further and speak it, pray it, or bless it over your child before she walks into the school every day. What my daughter and I like to do is pray on the way to school, and I say these truths over her as a blessing before she steps out of our vehicle. Then, when she gets nervous at school or hears a lie, she has already had these truths deposited into her mind and heart and can lean into them.

Reclaiming Identity

The physical battle plan has been created and implemented, the mental battlefield is continuing to be won, and the final camp to build is reclaiming and reinventing true identity. This may come easy for some kids; whereas others have been so shattered that they may not remember what lights them up. You are not going to allow your child to wave the surrender flag. Instead, together you are on a mission to find her true identity again. As bully survivor Aija Mayrock proclaims, "At the end of the day, the only person who can rob you of your dreams is you. Remember, success is a gift you give yourself."[33]

> "At the end of the day, the only person who can rob you of your dreams is you. Remember, success is a gift you give yourself."
> —Aija Mayrock

Now is the time to have your child open that "gift" of *her*. One way to do this is to make a list of her favorites using drawings or words. The first category is "at home." What does your child like to do inside, at home? Some examples of what children like to do at home are:

- Draw.
- Paint.
- Create with playdough or clay.
- Dance and sing.
- Role play: act out plays, dramatic play, puppets, etc.
- Make jewelry.
- Sew.
- Read.
- Journal.
- Build.

- Tinker and create.
- Play house.
- Pretend kitchen and chef/baker.
- Dress up as different jobs or people.
- Wrestle or "rough" play.

Then have your child move on to the next question: What does she like to do outdoors? This can cross over from inside to outside. So if the child is an older elementary age, a Venn diagram might be better for brainstorming, instead of a pictorial or written list. Here are examples of some favorite things to do outdoors:

- Ride a bicycle or scooter.
- Garden.
- Landscape.
- Use sidewalk chalk.
- Build forts, houses, or snow igloos.
- Play sports.
- Dance.
- Walk, jog, or run.
- Go on adventures.
- Skip, hop, or jump.
- Jump rope.
- Hula-hoop.
- Climb trees.
- Race other children on bicycles or on foot.
- Create music or play videos.
- Take pictures.

These are not exhaustive lists. Each child is unique and has her own likes, talents, giftings, and abilities. The key to this step is helping your child find what makes her uniquely her and start dabbling in that again. She does not have to do what she tries perfectly, but these activities can open her eyes to what she likes and remind her of what she is talented at again. This may not come naturally after being bullied, but encouraging her to try things on her lists or the lists above will help her find those things that will light her flame again. By trying these things, your child can start walking out these truths: *I am remarkably made, I am valuable, and I have a future.* This is when her hopelessness turns into *hope*! Speaking from experience, this hard work is worth it to see your child smile and shine again!!!

Once your child tries some of her favorite activities again, motivate her to do those things in public. Have her choose one of the items on her list and sign her up for a club, organization, sport, or volunteer activity, a place to grow in that gift. For example, my daughter loved to play basketball. Instead of signing her up for a competitive basketball team, we found the Christian organization Upward, where we knew the basketball coaches would be encouraging, pouring into her mentally, physically, and emotionally through verbal reinforcement, and where she could build back her confidence, as all children on the team get similar playing time. This is where her light began to shine brightly again.

After your child has taken these steps to find her true self, it is your job to celebrate the heck out of her and make her feel like a million bucks. Make each little and big step a *huge* deal! When she draws a picture that she is proud of, put it on the fridge, tape it to the place you put her artwork, or hang it in a frame. Then praise her for something specific in the drawing. For example, "I love the bright colors you used. Those colors brighten up the room," or "Those colors make me so happy." When she makes a goal on the soccer field, take her out for ice cream to celebrate and let the whole family congratulate her. If she builds a fort outside, ask her if you can have a picnic lunch inside it. Your praise

> **Make each little and big step your child takes toward finding herself a huge deal!**

and celebrating do not have to cost a penny, but they will mean the world to her as she learns to trust her true self again.

This celebration does not have to stay inside your family, either. Invite your "village." Ask grandparents, friends, neighbors, and whoever else is a safe person for your child to come alongside your child and acknowledge her achievements, big and small.

Talents, abilities, giftings, dreams, and your child's life are gifts to be unwrapped, unleashed, and celebrated by all!

> *Take a moment to take a deep breath in and a gentle breath out. You have walked through every door. Take in the weight of that! Were there times you didn't think you would make it out alive? Were there times when you wanted to wave the white flag of surrender? All those tear-stained moments, the screaming at the top of your lungs in frustration, and the nights of complete exhaustion were so worth it!*
>
> *Now is the time for you to roar like a mama lion. Now is the time to raise your sword. Stand tall with your sword in celebration, knowing the lies have been slain, the truth has taken its rightful place, and victory has been waged and won for your precious child! The victory is yours and hers, so relish the hard work it took. Your child is not a victim! Yell with me in victory, "My child is not a victim. My child is a SURVIVOR!!!" I am so proud of you! Imagine me sitting right next to you like a best friend would, tears rolling down my face, smiling from ear to ear, and proclaiming, "Well done, good and faithful servant. I am beyond proud of you, grateful that you invested the time to bring back your child's joy and identity, and excited she can now share her gifts and light with the world with a hope-filled future (that is what I am doing as I type this just for you). Please do not underestimate the power you hold as your child's primary advocate, love, and lifeline!*

I challenge you to take a picture of your child or of you standing next to her. Then print it out, frame it, and write the words, "I am _____." In the blank, write the truth that encompasses who your child is and what she now believes about herself. Next, have her say it out loud, proclaiming it each morning that she wakes up and shines her light into the world! I would be honored if you went one step further and emailed me a picture or posted it on social media with the hashtag #behindthehiddendoors.

It was a privilege to journey through these doors with you, to see your child come out victorious. You may flip the page and hear more about my daughter's victory and read more encouragement as you and your child walk in freedom!

Afterword

A Survivor's Testimony

As I sit down to write today, I am in awe of the journey we have traveled and how much my sweet Madison has overcome. This morning, my daughter woke up with a smile that stretched from ear to ear as we lavished her with a birthday breakfast full of her favorites: waffles and sizzling bacon. Her neighbor buddy and our little family sang, "Happy Birthday" to her while she blew out her candles and made a wish for year number twelve. She put on a beautiful outfit, brushed her teeth, braided her hair into piggy tales, placed her earrings just right, and joyfully giggled as she opened a few birthday presents from her siblings. Our house is filled with joy, laughter, and smiles! Wow! Saying that brings tears to my eyes; this moment was a long time coming!

If we flip back to the Introduction, you'll remember my daughter started in a dark place. Back then, she wouldn't have wanted to get up for the day, not even to celebrate her birthday, because she didn't believe she was worthy of being celebrated. When she finally did get up, her little body would have shuffled down the hall because she had lost all of her energy and strength during the night, especially with the nightmares she wrestled. A dark cloud followed her around wherever she went, and the words that came out of her mouth broke anyone's heart who heard them or crossed her path. Her brothers loved her, but they tried to avoid her at all costs so she wouldn't emotionally erupt all over them. In addition, she would have cared less what was on her plate for breakfast since she had no appetite, so few bites went in her mouth. It was a fight then to help her find the energy, desire, and mental strength to take care of the little things like personal hygiene. She believed no one liked her and that she was the worst person in the world!

Fast-forward to July 2022, one year after the bullying began. I remember this warm feeling so well. We were sitting in the counselor's office, and my daughter could not stop talking about the happiness in her life and the little events in her upcoming week, which she couldn't wait to experience. Her counselor even had to tell her that her session was almost up. She laughed as Madison speed-talked her way through her upcoming week. Her counselor looked at me, and I exclaimed, with tear-filled eyes, "Our girl is back! Her smile, her laughter, and her talkative self are back!" Then my eyes couldn't stop the floodgates as happy tears rushed down my face, and the counselor's eyes even moistened. Our sweet daughter had thrived alongside a gentle, kind-hearted, and brilliant counselor who found my daughter's buried light, cultivated it, and put it back on the lampstand to shine. That was the *first* best moment in our hard journey to healing.

The next best moment came on a January day in 2024 when Madison decided she was ready to start public school. To others, this didn't seem like much, but to her and this mama's heart, it was *huge*! You see, she had traveled the long, challenging two-year healing journey from being severely bullied by two girls in a private Christian school. She pushed through and released the trauma that had overtaken her mentally, psychologically, emotionally, and, a few times, physically. In addition, she learned to forgive the girls who targeted her day in and day out, not for their sake but for hers, so she could stand on her own two feet again. She grasped what it meant to forgive the adult staff who did not stand in the gap for her and keep her mentally and physically safe at school. Then, in turn, she opened up her heart and mind to trusting adults and leaders again—those who were not her parents.

The biggest feat she wrestled with daily (and still does today) is rewiring her brain to believe the truths God speaks over her and choosing to think and trust them as she *lives* and breathes. Man, human words have more power and weight than most give them credit!

My daughter just completed her first day of middle school at our local public school. These are the words I heard her say as she jumped in the car: "Mom, I had the best day. A girl in my first class asked if I wanted to sit by her. Then she showed me where all my other classes were. That's not even the best part, Mom. At lunch, she walked me through the hot lunch line even though she had cold lunch, and then guess what she said? 'Hey, do you wanna eat lunch with me and my friends?'"

This is what the healing journey is all about! Not just working through all the crud, but coming out on the other side as a victorious survivor, not a victim!

This is my daughter's and my hope for you and your child! May this book be a launching pad for you to find hope, identity, and healing. We want you to be victors on the other side, not waving your surrender flag but waving your victor's flag! We are not saying bad days won't happen again—because they will. Children are still human and can be mean and rude. However, now you and your child have the tools to navigate the trials to stand on your own feet in the identity, worth, belonging, hope, value, and love that only you possess.

To wrap up *Behind the Hidden Doors*, I have interviewed Madison, using the questions that offer the answers she wants everyone on their healing journey to hear. She wants other survivors to feel seen and heard. Additionally, she desires those on the survivor's team, from the parents to the teachers to the administrators, to hear her heart's cry for her generation and the generations to come.

Maybe someday she will write her own book, but for now, this is her voice, which she wants to share with those willing to listen and learn:

1. **What do you wish teachers or school staff would have done differently when you were getting bullied?**
   I wish they would have taken it more seriously and made it sound like it actually mattered. They just had me fill something out and acted like, Oh, here it goes again!

2. **What could the administration have done better to make you feel safer?**
   They could have made it not sound like it was my fault. They could have actually talked to her [the bully] and made her understand that it was not *okay and that she needed to not do that. And that she needed to stop and get her to a point that she understood how rude and hurtful it was.*

3. **Is there anything your parents could have done differently to support you?**
   No, I think my parents took care of it pretty well.

4. **What are you most grateful for that your parents did?**
   Probably that my mom got me a counselor so that I could talk through it and not be holding the feelings in.

5. **Are you glad you went to counseling? Why or why not?**
   Yes, 'cause the lady walked me through it very well and helped me understand that she [the bully] was being mean, and it wasn't necessarily my fault. She helped me feel valued and important.

6. **What was your initial reaction to going to the counselor?**
   I was scared and nervous and thought people would make fun of me because I needed help. Even though it was a really good thing that happened to me.

7. **What was your final emotion when you left your last counseling session?**

   I was grateful for all the help I got, and I was sad I wasn't going to get to see her again because she was really sweet.

8. **What strategies helped you the most in counseling?**

   The strategy that probably helped me the most was telling myself, every time she was rude, "You're beautiful. You're smart. You're kind." Just filling myself with positivity.

9. **What would you tell a child who is nervous to go to counseling?**

   There is no need to be nervous. It's okay to be nervous, but they are going to help you get through whatever you need to get through because their job is to help you feel valued.

10. **What qualities does a good counselor have?**

    A good counselor would be kind, sweet, and a good listener. They need to try to be good at understanding so that they can actually help you. If they can't understand and listen, then they aren't a good counselor because they can't problem-solve because they have to hear to help.

11. **How did you know you were ready to go to a school again instead of being homeschooled?**

    I knew I was ready because I felt more important. I felt good about myself. I was getting more socialized and feeling safe around other kids even when they were being rude. I felt safe to be able to handle it, walk away, and not stay in that emotion.

12. **What helps you before you go to school? What do you do or say before entering the school?**

    For me, it helps me to just tell myself all the good things in the day like, "This is going to be fun . . . and this is going to be fun." And just reading the Bible and hearing how God loves me and how He called us to be His own. Kind of getting myself feeling positive and valued and ready to go to school. So that when I am there, I am positive. I am like a positive bubble.

13. **What do you think or say at school to remind yourself that you are no longer a victim of bullying and are safe?**
    I remind myself there are security guards and there are people whose job it is to keep us feeling safe and feeling good. And I also remember that I know now, after not being bullied anymore, that some kids just have something going on with them, and they are bringing it out on other people even if they don't really know them. I remind myself that it is not necessarily me doing anything; it is just something they are going through.

14. **What do you think or say at school when someone is being mean?**
    Normally, I think this is not necessarily at me. It is just something they are saying then and not thinking through. What I normally say is, "This is not kind. It is not nice to be rude." [While] thinking or saying, I am not going to listen to this because it is rude.

15. **What is the best outcome that came out of being bullied?**
    I feel more positive in myself. I don't feel as much hate or anger when I get mad. I just feel more uplifted or positive.

16. **Who are you now? Complete this sentence: I am _____.**
    I am smart. I am beautiful. I am kind. I am a good leader. I am not a victim anymore. I am strong in my faith. I am just a more positive person.

17. **What do you want to say to a fellow bullying survivor?**
    *You are **valued**. You are **smart**. You are **beautiful**. You are **kind**. That kid [who] is being rude to you doesn't necessarily mean it at you. It doesn't mean you are doing anything wrong. It just*

means that kid is going through something hard, and they are taking it out on you. Don't dwell on it. Just let it go because they are not meaning it toward you.

Endnotes

1 "Measuring Student Safety: New Data on Bullying Rates at School." NCES Blog, Feb. 29, 2024, https://nces.ed.gov/blogs/nces/post/measuring-student-safety-new-data-on-bullying-rates-at-school.

2 Kuykendall, Sally. 2012. Bullying. Santa Barbara: Greenwood Publishing Group.

3 Ibid.

4 Ibid.

5 "What Is the Definition of Bullying?" BRIM, n.d., https://antibullyingsoftware.com/the-definition-of-bullying-for-kids/.

6 Kuykendall, Sally. 2012. Bullying. Santa Barbara: Greenwood Publishing Group.

7 Harber, Joel. 2007. Bullyproof Your Child for Life: Protect Your Child from Teasing, Taunting, and Bullying for Good. New York: Penguin Group.

8 Ibid.

9 Harber, Joel. 2007. Bullyproof Your Child for Life: Protect Your Child from Teasing, Taunting, and Bullying for Good. New York: Penguin Group.

10 Ibid.

11 Ibid.

12 Ibid.

13 Smith, Christina. 2022. Personal Communication.

14 Whitson, Signe. 2014. 8 Keys to End Bullying: Strategies for Parents & Schools. New York: W.W. Norton & Company.

15 Ibid.

16 Ibid.

17 Ibid.

18 Ibid.

19 Bazelon, Emily. 2013. Sticks and Stones: Defeating the Culture of Bullying. New York: Random House.

20 Ibid.

21 Ibid.

22 Harber, Joel. 2007. Bullyproof Your Child for Life :Protect Your Child from Teasing, Taunting, and Bullying for Good. New York: Penguin Group.

23 Ibid.

24 Whitson, Signe. 2014. 8 Keys to End Bullying: Strategies for Parents & Schools. New York: W.W. Norton & Company.

25 Harber, Joel. 2007. Bullyproof Your Child for Life :Protect Your Child from Teasing, Taunting, and Bullying for Good. New York: Penguin Group.

26 Ibid.

27 Whitson, Signe. 2014. 8 Keys to End Bullying: Strategies for Parents & Schools. New York: W.W. Norton & Company.

28 Allen, Jennie. 2024. Untangle Your Emotions: Naming What You Feel and Knowing What to Do About It. New York: Penguin Random House.

29 Ibid.

30 Mayrock, Aija. 2015. The Survival Guide to Bullying. Singapore: Scholastic Inc.

31 Ibid.

32 Ibid.

33 Ibid.

GET CONNECTED DEEPER!

Scan to learn and discover more about Author Rachel Rector

About the Author

Rachel Rector is a coauthor of the Barnes and Noble best-selling women's devotional *More than Enough: The Silent Struggle of a Woman's Identity*. Before becoming a best-selling author, she was an educator who advocated for her students for fourteen years, teaching in several grades from preschool to twelfth grade, in three states.

Two of Rachel's four children were bullied in the school system; one situation was quickly resolved since she knew the fast-action steps to take. The other involved a year of heartbreak as she tried to advocate without knowing the helpful steps, which she shares in this book. Because of her experience, Rachel has been in roles as both the parent advocate for her children in public and private schools and as the professional teacher, jumping through all the legal and professional hoops to make sure the students in all her classrooms felt seen, heard, and safe among their peers and the staff who taught them.

Rachel is mostly known for her God-given gift of mercy, helping everyone she meets feel seen, heard, and valued. A common phrase she hears is, "I do not know why I shared all that with you. I have never shared that before." She is on a mission in her home, her blog, her books, and anywhere God leads her next to help females and children reclaim hope, identity, and joy in life.

Rachel was born and raised in the Midwest, but she has always had a heart for the beach and the ocean. During the writing of *Behind the Hidden Doors*, she moved her whole family cross-country to Virginia Beach, Virginia. While soaking up the sunshine, she continues to be a compassionate encourager and trailblazer as she walks in her newest calling of being a freedom activator for women and children.

Recommended Resources

Books for Parents

Praying for Boys, by Brooke McGlothlin. This resource gives ideas for how to build character traits and rebuild a boy's identity using verses from the Bible. McGlothilin additionally provides sample Scripture-based prayers to pray over the boy in your life.

Praying for Girls, by Teri Lynne Underwood. This book was inspired by the Praying for Boys book as the author heard moms request a version for girls. As a girl-mom herself, Underwood gives more ideas on how to help your female child when building back her identity, worth, and value. In addition, it provides sample prayers to pray over your daughter and activities to do with her to enforce the identity reinventing.

Unstick Your Mind, by Mimika Cooney. As a leading Christian mindset coach and author, Cooney shares her experience with overwhelm, burnout, and trying to get out of a negative mindset. This book is for parents, or any adult, choosing to renew their minds during their healing journeys. She shares how "words are containers of power. We need to know the importance of what we're saying and how we're saying it [to ourselves mentally and our children verbally]." There is power in our nonverbal and verbal words, and we can choose to use them for life or death.

Untangle Your Emotions, by Jennie Allen. As stated in this book, "This book is worth thousands of dollars of counseling." It will help you navigate all the emotions you and your child are feeling. Additionally, it will give you practical tips on what to do with the emotions when they rise up or return. She wrote a wonderful companion book, Get Out of Your Head. I had the pleasure of being on the launch team for the second book, and I can say from experience, it will bless you and your healing journey (it sure did me!).

Books for Children

Rise Up Beautiful, Girls Edition, by Sandra L. Coates. This workbook is great for upper elementary girls and older who want to discover or reclaim their identity, confidence, purpose, and value. Additionally, Coates has begun a movement called United + TRU that connects girls from all over the nation who want to live T-Transformed, R-Redeemed, U-Unique. I have partnered with United + TRU to volunteer with their role models and speakers for their amazing fashion show here locally.

The Survival Guide to Bullying, by Aija Mayrock. This resource is written by a teen bullying survivor for teens. The child hears this teen author explain different types of bullying, all the emotions the survivor feels, the reality that happens while being bullied, coping strategies, and how to reclaim identity again. I use quotes, coping strategies, tools for reclaiming identity, and a battle plan for going back into the school. I highly recommend this for any preteen and above who is being bullied, or has been.

You Are Not Alone, by Jennie Allen. This book is the children's guide version of her book, *Untangle Your Emotions*. Allen does an excellent job of walking through the negative beliefs others, such as bullies, have placed on children, the thoughts and emotions that go with each belief, and how to effectively flip the script and walk in truth. She tackles the common fears and negative beliefs this generation of children are walking through on a daily basis. She meets children where they are, helps them feel seen and heard, and empowers them to walk in truth. This is a must-have for upper elementary children and above. For the younger children, the adult can read the book and teach the children the truth.

Websites

National Cyber Security Alliance (NCSA) (www.staysafeonline.org): A nonprofit organization that provides digital information, resources, and tools for children, adults, and businesses on how to effectively navigate and use the internet safely.

National Suicide Prevention Lifeline 1-800-273-TALK (www.suicidepreventionlifeline.org)

Stop Bullying (www.stopbullying.gov): An official government website that offers information on how to stop or prevent bullying for all ages, and from students to school administrators. In addition, it shares what bullying laws and policies are supposed to be upheld in each state. You can search your state and see what your child's school should be implementing.

STOP Cyberbullying (www.stopcyberbullying.org): This was the first cyberbullying prevention program created in North America. It has specially trained young volunteers who design and deliver community programs to help their peers address cyberbullying.

Have you found yourself declaring
Why me?
Why this?
Why now?
There's got to be more than this...

This podcast is for the woman who is ready to break free from the chains of your past, step into the radiant light of your true self, and begin your journey to freedom!

Tune in to Freedom Diaries: The Untold, Unbreakable Stories of Hope to Unleash Identity, Purpose, Joy and Worth!

Through storytelling and hope-dealing - we will open the long-locked diaries of women who have been tried by fire and came out radiant. They journeyed through the struggle/pain to come out victorious as their refined new self. They fought to no longer be bound by their past, but instead willingly jumped into the freedom of their present and future self. These stories all bond each of us together as we all need freeing from something in our life.

Are you ready to take the first step towards your freedom?

Primary Bedroom Door

Now's the time

to Replace the Lies Spoken Over your Child, and ARMOR UP by filling your child's mind with truth.

Grab Rachel's Spiritual Affirmation Cards HERE!

Finding joy in God and breaking out of the boxes the world puts us in!

Discover More Than Enough: The Silent Struggle of a Women's Identity - A Women's Devotional Cohort with Rachel Rector!

Order your copy today!
Bible Study and Curriculum are also available for your Women's Group Today, co-written by Rachel

Your story doesn't just matter for you, it matters to move others!

1 CHRONICLES 16:24 (NLT)
*Publish His glorious deeds among the nations.
Tell everyone about the amazing things he does.*

A Christian Publishing House dedicated to turning messages into movements. On mission to mobilize the critical voices for such a time as this. Specializing in co-hort compilations, to make way for writers to collaborate with other prolific members of the Body of Christ. Our works open conversations around mental, physical, relational, financial and spiritual health and wholeness journeys, often directly associated to our rooted identity and purpose driven life.

Learn More & Don't Wait to Get Published!

Thank You

Thank You For Reading My Book!

I really appreciate all of your feedback, and I love hearing what you have to say.

I need your input to make the next version of this book and my future books even better.

Please leave me a helpful review on Amazon letting me know what you thought of the book.

Thank you so much!
Rachel Rector

www.ingramcontent.com/pod-product-compliance
Lightning Source LLC
Chambersburg PA
CBHW060606080526
44585CB00013B/705